Dave Courtney's Heroes and Villains

by Dave Courtney

Virgin books has no control over, does not endorse, support or
assume any liability or responsibility for the contents or views
expressed in any websites, articles or any other publications
or materials referred to in this book.

First published in Great Britain in 2005 by
Virgin Books Ltd
Thames Wharf Studios
Rainville Road
London
W6 9HA

Copyright © Dave Courtney 2005

The right of Dave Courtney to be identified as the Author of
this Work has been asserted by him in accordance with the
Copyright, Designs and Patents Act, 1988.

This book is sold subject to the condition that it shall not,
by way of trade or otherwise, be lent, resold, hired out or
otherwise circulated without the publisher's prior written
consent in any form of binding or cover other than that in
which it is published and without a similar condition including
this condition being imposed on the subsequent purchaser.

A catalogue record for this book is available from the
British Library.

ISBN 1 185227 254 6

The paper used in this book is a natural, recyclable
product made from wood grown in sustainable forests.
The manufacturing process conforms to the regulations
of the country of origin.

Printed and bound in Italy

PICTURE CREDITS
DAVE'S OWN: 2/3, 5, 7, 8/9, 10/11, 84/85, 92/93, 132/133, 134/135, 139, 140/141, 163 (top), 171; CORBIS: 1, 14, 15, 18/19, 21, 22, 23, 25 (both), 26/27, 28/29, 30/31, 32, 34/35, 36, 42/43, 60, 62, 63, 68, 80, 81, 82/3,94/95, 96/97, 98, 100/101, 104/105, 118/119, 120, 121 (both), 123, 124/125, 126, 128, 129, 131/132, 158/159,160, 162 (both), 163 (bottom middle/bottom right), 164/165, 166/177, 168, 169 (both), 170, 172/173; EMPICS: 86/87, 88, 90, 107, 108/109, 112, 142/143, 144, 148/149; GETTY: 33, 49, 51; KOBAL: 12/13, 16, 17, 38 (both), 40/41, 44, 54, 55, 56, 57, 58/59, 64, 65, 66, 70 (both), 73,74/75, 76, 78, 79, 102/103, 106; PHOTONEWS: 110, 115 (top), 130 (both), 136/137, 147, 150/151, 152, 153 (both), 154, 155, 156/157; REX FEATURES: 46/47; TOPFOTO: 146.

contents

INTRODUCTION	06
HEROES	10
Al Capone	12
Rocky Sullivan	20
Rico Bandello	28
Don Corleone	36
Tony Montana	44
Henry Hill	52
Neil McCauley	60
Vincent Vega	68
Big Chris	76
Dave Malone	84
VILLAINS	92
The Krays	94
The Richardsons	102
Joey Pyle	110
John Gotti	118
Bruce Reynolds	126
Roy Shaw & Lenny McLean	134
Freddie Foreman	142
Charles Bronson	150
Howard Marks	158
Ronnie Biggs	166
EPILOGUE	174
INDEX	176

Hello! I'm Dave Courtney.

Well that's the introductions over, let's get on with the book. No? All right then, here's a little DVD extra…

When I started thinking about this book, I came up with all sorts of names. Darth Vader, the Daleks, Winston Churchill, Idi Amin, the old woman who lived in a shoe – she was fucking scary, I kid you not. But eventually I narrowed it down to this lot. Ten people I'm proud to call heroes and ten who are very definitely villains.

So, what's it all about? Well, the ten people I've chosen as heroes are pretty much characters from the movies who any aspiring gangster would do well to look at and go, 'I am not worthy, thank you for teaching me.' They're all fucking top drawer, premier division characters who absolutely sew up their chosen field. There's one real life character in there, too – the guy who was arguably the inspiration for a lot of these films. His name is Alphonse Capone – you might have heard of him. I decided to put him in the Hero section cos he actually died before I was born and although I've heard and read every story about the cunt, he's no more real to me than Scarface or Vincent Vega from Pulp Fiction. You understand what I'm saying? So when I read about him having 2,000 coppers on his books in Chicago and it's actually before World War Two, I go, 'That's a great story.' All the chaps in the Villains section, on the other hand, are proper hardcore premier division naughty boys. And apart from one of them, I know them all very well (and the one I don't, I know the Family of, if you get what I mean). And the thing is, if you're gonna split hairs then it's hard to say that these villains ain't heroes, cos they most genuinely are. And what's more, they're either all alive today or have been alive in my lifetime, so they're proper News at Ten characters. You've all heard about them, you've all seen them in the papers – fuck, half of you have been robbed by them!

My point is that everyone's got a little bit of hero and villain in them. When you're kids, you play cowboys and Indians thinking it is really simple: the cowboys were the goodies and the Red Indians the baddies. That's the myth. We grow up to learn that it weren't really like that. Same deal when you play cops and robbers. It all seems so simple. Goodies against baddies. But real life ain't that black and white. There's a fuck load of grey in the middle. So what the twenty-odd geezers in this book are, are good baddies – or bad goodies. It depends which way you're looking at it. That's definitely how I see myself – and I'm not alone.

There's an American metal band called Rancid who have actually recorded a song called 'Dave Courtney: England's Robin Hood', and actually I've got a lot of time for the cunt. Apart from the Lincoln green tights, he was everything you'd want to be. A good shot, loved by the masses and a dead cert when it came to getting some from Maid Marion. Talk about a good baddy! Robin Hood definitely falls into that category. Just cos he does something that pisses off a few corrupt wealthy landowners, that don't mean he's a prick. The actual ending to Robin Hood was mindblowing, though, wasn't it? Richard the Lionheart comes home from the Crusades, slaps the Sheriff and Prince John and they all lived happily ever after – that could only happen 50 million years ago, or whenever it was. Maid Marion didn't shag anyone else in the woods, Robin was the best bow and arrower, there was chivalry among men, the underdog won, he robbed from the rich to give to the poor and no fucker took the mickey out of his Lincoln green tights. Message: keep with the masses, keep moral right on your side and you'll live forever. (That's how the IRA get away with robbing banks, cos they're doing it for the cause.) Oh, and men shouldn't wear tights and short skirts, especially if their cock is as big as Errol Flynn's. But thank fuck they've found Robin Hood's tree in Sherwood Forest. I was worried there for a minute.

Every little player that I feature in this book has been given a rating on my duster-o-meter. The thing is, these geezers are all up there as far as I'm concerned. The only reason they're in here is because I think they're the bollocks. Against any other name they'd all be fives, but it's only cos I'm choosing between them for you lot out there that we're being a bit picky. On a normal day they would score maximum points in all the competitions: Mr Universe, Baddy of the Year, Crufts, Masterchef, you name it. So where I've given marks out of five, it's all relative to each other. Got it? Good. Or else you're staying behind for detention.

I'll tell you a secret, though, and it's this: when I was asked to put this list together I think I said two words: 'Fuck' and 'off'. Why would I write a book about loads of other cunts when I could be writing about yours truly? But then they said, 'Dave, you could impart some of your own messages in the articles on each character – if you're clever, it could be as much about you as about them.' And now you're fucking talking! So what you're about to read is me telling you about someone I like or admire, and sprinkled within each chapter are a few nuggets of information or truths that you can use in your own lives. I know you're happier now.

Basically what these films and my book are, are encyclopaedias of information disguised as entertainment. They portray things in a way that you will remember. If you're sitting in school and your history teacher is banging on about stuff that happened in 1066, the only thing you'll remember is the date. If someone's sitting there giving you facts and figures, it's not going to sink in. But if they told you a joke and it was fucking funny, and within that joke was actually a story, you'd remember that joke and the lesson for a million years. That's what people do with films, they get the story out and hidden in it is what they really want to say. And this book is the same.

This ain't by any means the complete list, cos every man's got enough heroes to fill a dozen books, and there's loads of geezers who miss out this time such as Che Guevara. This bloke attacked America with just seventeen men, a Frank Spencer hat and a fucking dinghy. That's stuff to wank over, that is. For a naughty man, he was the bees'. He broke into prisons just as his mates was gonna get firing squad'd, busted them out then ran off into the sunset. He was pretty impressive when he was working for Castro, but when he was just a guerrilla taking on the world, he was fucking awesome. He was a hero to thousands.

Pablo Escobar's another one. His story is magic, it's got so much excitement in it. Every schoolboy, every criminal who wants to be a gangster, that is what they're striving for. Someone who's in a country small enough to actually have his own army and the real government is bribed to do what he wants. How dreamy is that? He's got helicopters and tanks and ships of his own and he is actually a king in his own country. As villains go, how close to being perfect does he come?

Legs Diamond, John Dillinger, Bluebeard, Jesse James, 'Baby Face' Nelson, 'Pretty Boy' Floyd, Ned Kelly, Albert Chapman, Tony Lambrianou, Wilf Pine, Geoff Maxwell, Cas Pennant, Bernie Davies, Ian Freeman, Dave Ford, Eamon O'Keefe, Robert Maxwell, Simon Cowell – the list of genuine villains goes on and on. But they're all for another day. What you've got here is Dave Courtney's personal collection of reprobates and radicals, naughty boys and ne'er do wells, heroes and villains. En-fucking-joy it, now, won't you?

DAVE COURTNEY OBE

Heroes

Al Capone

FACTS

AL CAPONE (1899-1947)

DAVE'S CRIME FILE
God to some and devil to others, Al Capone was the original American gangster. Starting out as a bar-room bouncer, where he picked up the knife wounds that earned him the nickname 'Scarface', he went on to run the racketeering of early 20th century Chicago and was the first criminal to realize the value of having politicians and policemen in his pocket. He rigged elections, removed opposition candidates and passionately 'encouraged' voters to put a cross in his candidate's box, all for a blind eye turned towards his other business. He was also the first criminal since Robin Hood to openly divert his earnings to looking after the poor.

DAVE'S DODGY DOSSIER
He clubbed two blokes to death with a baseball bat and he was chucked out of school in the sixth grade for attacking his teacher, but Al Capone's most famous bit of naughtiness was the St Valentine's Day Massacre on 14 February 1929, where his men dressed as coppers and shot seven of Bugsy Moran's men in a warehouse.

ANYTHING YOU SAY WILL BE TAKEN DOWN…
When I sell liquor, it's called bootlegging; when my patrons serve it on Lake Shore Drive, it's called hospitality.

In that era it was men fighting for the right to have a drink, and Capone was leading the fight.

Growing up in England in the '50s and '60s, we had all these mythical heroes to look up to. There was knights in shining armour, cowboys taking on the Indians single-handed, pirates jolly rogering anything that moved – and flash American gangsters. The only difference was, the gangsters we were pretending to be were real. Just cos they was in another country and the stories sounded so far-fetched compared to what we had over here, it was easy to forget that. But it was true, it really happened, and one geezer was more real than the rest.

To a young Englishman, Al Capone epitomized the word 'gangster'. In that era it was men fighting for the right to have a drink, and Capone was leading the fight. By the time he was 26, he had 1,000 gunmen on his books and a weekly wage bill of $300,000. It's safe to imagine he weren't short of a few bob if that's what he was handing out, and in fact, in the 1960s, The Guinness Book of Records had him down as holding the record for the highest personal income in the world. And that's based on what they knew about, if you know what I mean. Obviously he couldn't admit he was a villain so he actually listed his trade in official papers as 'second-hand furniture dealer'. How mental is that? The richest geezer in the States is an old Steptoe.

Of course, it never hurts to have a few different business cards and different strings to your bow. As well as being an author, comedian, actor, director, singer and fucking dwarf-juggler if that's what people want, I'm also a journalist and I've got an NUJ union card to prove it. I only use it to wind the authorities up cos this card gives me Access All Areas in courtrooms. When they're making controversial legal decisions and they throw the jury out and move all the gallery to the canteen, I'm allowed to sit there and there's fuck all they can do about it. I walk in and out of court cases and the coppers go, 'That's Dave Courtney.' It's mental.

The other little thing I've got is my OBE. Did you know it's actually illegal to put 'OBE' after your name unless you actually have one? So a few years ago I bought one. The geezer wasn't needing it anymore, so I've got it at home next to my war medals, boxing trophies and library ticket. And get this: if you write to Tony Blair at 10 Downing Street, he has to, by law, send you a reply. So I do this all the time, cos I cannot tell you how dreamy it is to get a letter from the Prime Minister, the geezer whose boys have been trying to shut me down for ten years, and it starts: 'Dear Mr Courtney, OBE.' What a flash cunt.

And speaking of them, that's why we all loved Capone. He was classily flamboyant, like Muhammad Ali. He didn't live in some shitty council house with his parents like the Krays; he took a suite at the fucking Waldorf Hotel for him and all his boys. He didn't run around hiding from the police; he had half the Chicago force on his payroll. This is the man who once hit the Mayor of Cicero on the steps of City Hall and hundreds of Old Bill just looked the other way – just like what happened to me when I smacked the bent copper Austin Warnes at the Old Bailey. When Capone took his seat at a baseball game they'd cheer his name louder than the team – which right pissed off people like Herbert Hoover, who was often there as well. So it weren't long before he found himself in a position where it was a waste of time being low key. So, seeing there was nothing he could do to stop them looking at him, he might as well be as colourful as possible. I can understand that, cos if I wore a tweed suit, drove a Mini Metro and lived down an alley in fucking Sidcup, the police would still be looking at me. So considering they are monitoring me anyway, I'll give them something to look at with the paintings on the side of the house and all that.

Al Capone might have had the Rolls-Royce, the sharp suits, the best champagne, the cigars, the real trappings of an A-list celebrity, but he weren't afraid to share it, and that's what won

By the time he was 26 he had 1,000 gunmen on his books and a weekly wage bill of $300,000.

When I went to Cannes to promote my film Hell to Pay, the paparazzi couldn't get enough of these 70-odd geezers pitching up in the sharpest black gangster threads that I'd bought them. **DAVE**

him the public support. Like every businessman, he had his expense account and he did it properly. He always put people up in the best hotels, he always picked them up in the Roller, took them to shows, got them laid. He was the perfect host and that's how I consider myself. He ran gambling, prostitution and boot-legging, which if you think about it, was basically giving the people what they wanted. And even if people couldn't afford it, he didn't forget them. Capone was the first person in Chicago to open free 'soup kitchens' at the beginning of the Great Depression, cos he knew the value of keeping the masses onside when he was being so public in his naughtiness. He even handed out second-hand clothes to down and outs, so even tramps was running around in tasty old Crombies an' that.

And, because he kept it classy like that, it was very easy for someone over in England to look at Capone and not see all the bad things, but just want the lifestyle. I've learnt a lot off the way he did business and I'll tell you something he did that I thought was so wicked that I actually done it years later. He bought 50 brand new Crombies, 50 brand new black suits and 50 brand new pairs of shoes, all identical, for his top boys. So when he went out, they all looked the bollocks and he had the best-dressed army of hard-nuts in the world. And I did exactly the same. When I went to Cannes to promote my film, Hell to Pay, the paparazzi couldn't get enough of these 70-odd geezers pitching up in the sharpest black gangster threads that I'd bought them. Unfortunately, the shop didn't have as many as I wanted – they was one short – so I had to wear this wicked white one which made me stand out a little bit in that crowd. What a shame that was!

Speaking of black and white, that's actually another little thing he and I have in common, although the authorities have tried to stop it getting out in both our cases, cos it makes us look a bit too nice. But Al Capone was probably the first equal opportunity mobster employer. He didn't care if a geezer was black, Jewish, Irish, had four arms or was a midget like Frankie Fraser: if he was trustworthy he was in. That's pretty unheard of in a lot of modern businesses, which is disgusting to me, cos in my life I know I've been responsible for bringing together gangsters of every denomination. When people see Dave Courtney was married to a Jamaican bird for fourteen years, a few of them have had to change the way they look at people like that. I am friends with the Yardies, the Triads, the IRA, the Eastern European mob, the Italians in New York – they might not get on with each other, but they all like Dave.

No one ever lives up to their myth, not Dave Courtney, Ronnie Kray or Mother Theresa, but with Al Capone you really want him to. He was proper leader material, a bit nutty, but he weren't afraid to get his hands dirty and he looked after his own. He was also ahead of his time when it came to the psychology side of crime. Once, he threw a banquet to honour two of his generals, John Scalise and Albert Anselmi, but when they turned up he bashed their brains in with an Indian club for betraying him. But as usual, he was clever, cos he knows if he'd done it on his own somewhere, someone would have had something to say about it. All the whispers would start and he'd get shafted. But cos he's done it in front of everyone, if you grass him up you have to admit you was there and involved in it. 'Wow, he's just done that with a bat and I never stopped him.'

At the end of the day, though, cos he had so many people in his pocket, the authorities could never get Capone for murder or being a gangster or anything like that. So they did what they still do now. Think of it this way: if I didn't like you, I wouldn't want my friends to like you either, and the police are no different. If they can't get you they have a word with your bank manager, local traffic wardens, your kids' headmaster and the Inland Revenue, and between them they'll find a way to slow you

So what happened to Capone was the tax man had a close look at the accounts of America's richest second-hand furniture salesman and decided there were a few irregularities and off he went to Alcatraz for tax evasion.

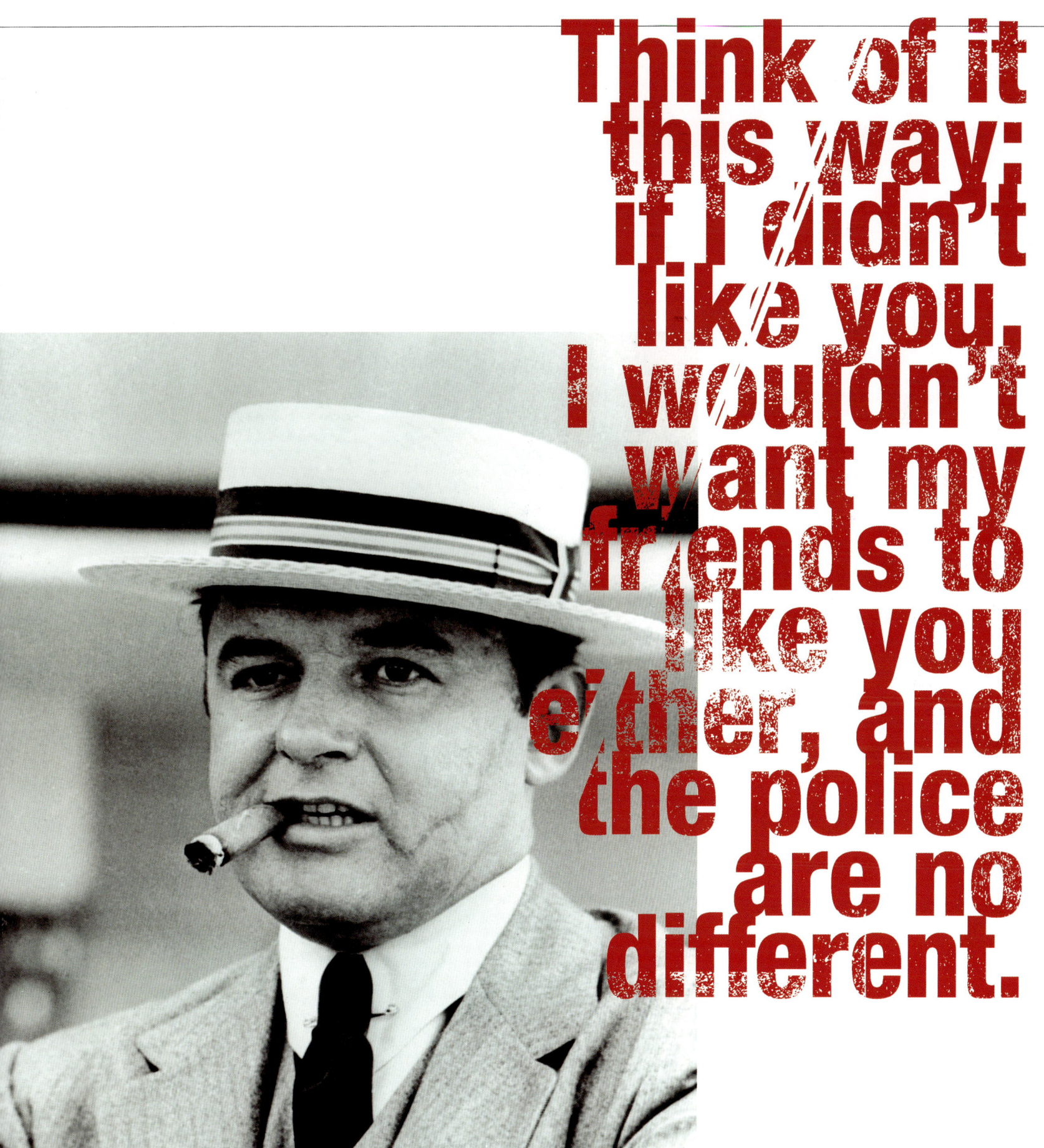

Think of it this way: if I didn't like you, I wouldn't want my friends to like you either, and the police are no different.

down somehow. So what happened to Capone was the tax man had a close look at the accounts of America's richest second-hand furniture salesman and decided there were a few irregularities and off he went to Alcatraz for tax evasion.

But the authorities knew that they could only hold him for a few years and then he'd be out running the country again, so they were a bit naughty, if you ask me. What they done was this. When he went into Alcatraz, Capone had syphilis and the authorities knew how bad it was and what medication he needed. But if you check the medical records they have at the prison, and I've done the tour, I've seen them myself, you'll see that everyone else who suffered the same thing got one drug, and he got something else. They actually deliberately allowed his syphilis to get to a stage where it couldn't be controlled before he was given the right pills. How wicked is that? But he's still a fucking hero.

AND THE MORAL IS...
It's nice to be important but important to be nice. Al Capone had the whole of Chicago queuing up to hide him from the authorities. People will always do more for you if they like you than if they're scared of you.

Rocky Sullivan
by James Cagney

FACTS
JAMES CAGNEY ANGELS WITH DIRTY FACES (1938)

DAVE'S FILM FACTS
Directed by Michael Curtiz. Written by Rowland Brown, John Wesley, Warren Duff and Ben Hecht and Charles MacArthur (both uncredited). Directed by Casablanca helmer Curtiz, Angels With Dirty Faces tells the story of Rocky and Jerry, two kids growing up in New York's notorious Hell's Kitchen area. Years later Rocky turns to racketeering while Jerry signs up as a priest who is anxious to stop street urchins turning out like his friend. Also featuring Humphrey Bogart, the film portrayed James Cagney's mesmerising turn as the archetypal Capone-esque gangster Rocky Sullivan.

ANYTHING YOU SAY WILL BE TAKEN DOWN…
'Morning, gentlemen. Nice day for a murder.'

DAVE'S DUSTER-O-METER
INFLUENCE 5
LEADERSHIP 4
SUCCESS 3
NAUGHTINESS 4
AUTHENTICITY 3

Stop any gangster in the street (go on, I dare you) and ask him who are his heroes and James Cagney's name will be up the top of that list.

When you operate in the cosy world of the police, everything is easier to understand if it's black and white (with maybe a bit of flashing blue to brighten things up). So, in their little brains, they think all villains are evil and all coppers have the sun shining full beam out of their arses. The truth is, there's a million shades of grey in between, but cos that don't help them with their paperwork, the Old Bill choose to ignore it. They won't admit there's such a thing as a bad goody or a good baddy. But there is, of course there is, and I should know, cos I'm one of them, and this geezer was as well.

Stop any gangster in the street (go on, I dare you) and ask him who are his heroes, and James Cagney's name will be up the top of that list. And this is why. Cagney, in all of his films, even though he played different characters, always portrayed a man with a heart. He was the original lovable rogue, with a bullet for any bastard and a dollar for the down-and-out in the gutter. He was the Dave Courtney of the old black and white world cos he was a romantic and he never let you forget that all the bad things he did was just business. The thing is this: being a gangster is just a job, like being a plumber. You don't walk around the house carrying a violin case in full spats and Crombie 24/7. You don't open fire on your missus if she burns your toast, or wear a balaclava to kiss her goodnight – you might ask her to, but that's another story. Being a criminal is not like that, is it? And Cagney's characters were all just normal blokes who happened to have a naughty job.

Even though they was all the same really, the part that makes anyone in the gangster fraternity tip their trilbies to Cagney was Rocky Sullivan in Angels With Dirty Faces. Imagine saying for real, 'Morning gentlemen. Nice day for a murder.' That's proper underworld wank material, that is. But he didn't just make that persona up and you don't have to be Sherlock Holmes to work out who he based it on. I've been to Chicago and Alcatraz, I've done the 'Scarface' tours and gone 'Wow' at all the statistics of all the naughty things Al Capone done, but what's not really said is what a nice bloke he was – and that's the bit Cagney gets down to a T. Why the police cosied up to him, why people let him in their clubs for nothing, why half the city hid him from the police when he was in trouble – it was all cos he was a nice bloke who was just basically 'one of us'. And it's amazing how far that will get you. Thousands will forgive you killing loads of people on St Valentine's Day as long as at the end of it you sent your missus a bunch of flowers.

I have actually made a record called 'The Ten Commandments', and part of the chorus has one of my catchphrases on it: it's nice to be important, but it's important to be nice. And that was Capone and Cagney's characters all over. And like Capone, whose reputation got destroyed by the press in the end, now I'm in a position where the media are told, 'Don't say nothing nice about Courtney.' I can see that in years to come people will look at the official clippings and think I'm a horrible cunt. I can't blame them, because that's the way they make sure I'm reported. According to the authorities' records, the only pictures of me are outside the Old Bailey in sharp suits giving it all that. You won't see me sitting here with my bollocks hanging out my pants bunging my neighbour twenty quid so he can pay his gas bill. That would fuck up their black and white image of me as that nasty bit of work, wouldn't it?

What the police don't realize, though, is that there's always gonna be villains. (Considering 50 per cent of the country's jobs are based on maintaining law and order to some extent, England would actually be fucked if all naughty boys decided to pack up their shooters and open B&Bs in Blackpool.) And if you're gonna be a villain anyway, it makes sense to want to be like Jimmy Cagney, cos he was such a fucking good advert for that type of flashy

> **He was the original lovable rogue, with a bullet for any bastards and a dollar for the down-and-out in the gutter.**

American gangster. He made a whole world of people think criminals was always nicely dressed and they looked after their ma.

He did it so successfully that everyone I know thinks they're the new Rocky Sullivan. No one likes to confess they're a 'bad' baddy, do they? We all like to think we are, or hope the public perceives us as, a good one. But without a doubt, it was a lot easier in them days than it is now to be like that. I'm afraid it's so cut-throat out there today and, with the financial rewards of the narcotics industry being as big as they are, there's no room for sentiment or loyalty if you want to survive. All that hand-on-heart Three Musketeers 'all for one and one for all' business got washed out when the white powder started arriving by the truckload.

Everyone can do a Cagney impression, can't they? 'You dirty rat' and 'I'm a Yankee doodle dandy' and all that. But there's another reason why he's so popular, and this is a funny one but it's true: James Cagney made such a believable gangster cos he was little. He weren't some flat-nosed, walking, grunting bicep, and he weren't that good-looking, neither, he was just this normal little bloke. And let's face it, there's more little people than big people out there, so of course everyone's gonna be rooting for him. In fact, when you look at war leaders through history, the actual people who were really doing it were all midgets: Winston Churchill, Adolf Hitler, Genghis fucking Khan, Napoleon, Nelson, Chairman Mao, Pol Pot, Mussolini, Stalin, Lenin – they were all tiny. Makes you think, don't it?

Even though Rocky was only a little bleeder, he actually stood up for the ones even littler than him – the kids – which is another reason you have to love the guy. Angels With Dirty Faces is probably my favourite old gangster film, and that's because the ending's out of this fucking world. Rocky takes the rap for all his mates and has to go to the electric chair. The vicar giving the last rites, his mate Father Jerry says, 'You have to scream and shout like you're

> The Old Bill won't admit there's such a thing as a bad goody or a good baddy. But there is, of course there is, and I should know, cos I'm one of them, and this geezer was as well. **DAVE**

scared or all of these kids will follow in your footsteps and want to be like you.' But now he's got a problem, ain't he? Cos all the chaps are listening in as well and he'll look a right pillock to them if he turns on the waterworks. So what does he do? What's more important? Keeping his gang happy and not looking like a coward, or stopping all these kids getting Frenchfried like him? You have no idea what he's going to do, and when it actually came to it, he pretended to cry. You can't watch that scene without going, 'Go on, James, you the man. Go on Jamesey.' Top bloke.

The only downer I have with that ending is it makes you realize how crap things are these days. Now he'd grass all his mates up rather than go to the chair. It's the same as my all-time favourite film, Spartacus. That is a story of love, of being the underdog, sticking together, beating the odds. And that's totally Dave Courtney, that's how I live my life. So when Kirk Douglas gets caught they all go, 'I'm Spartacus' to stop him going down. But now they'd go, 'He's Spartacus. I'm Kevin, that's Colin, we know him. The bloke you want's over there behind that bush. I can see his leg.'

AND THE MORAL IS...
Don't judge a crook by his cover. Villainy's a nine-to-five job, the same as any other – nine at night till five in the morning. A plumber ain't a plumber when he's got his feet up watching EastEnders or he's seeing to his missus, and a gangster's no different. Just cos you're a cunt during the day don't mean you pull the wings off butterflies at home.

Rico Bandello
by Edward G Robinson

FACTS
EDWARD G ROBINSON LITTLE CAESAR (1931)

DAVE'S FILM FACTS
Directed by Mervyn LeRoy. Written by W.R. Burnett, Francis Edward Faragoh, Robert Lee, Robert Lord and Darryl F. Zanuck. Edward G. Robinson is bad baddy Caesar Enrico Bandello, in what was considered the prototype gangster movie of the talkie era (the first talkie was Lights of New York). A rags-to-(other people's) riches story, it shows the rapid success of the over-ambitious Rico as he becomes a crime lord. Such was the impact of Robinson's evil character, the federal anti-organized crime law – The Racketeering Influence Corrupt Organisation Act, or RICO – was named after him. More importantly, he was also the inspiration for Porky Pig and Chief Wiggum in The Simpsons.

ANYTHING YOU SAY WILL BE TAKEN DOWN…
'If you want me, you'll have to come and get me!'

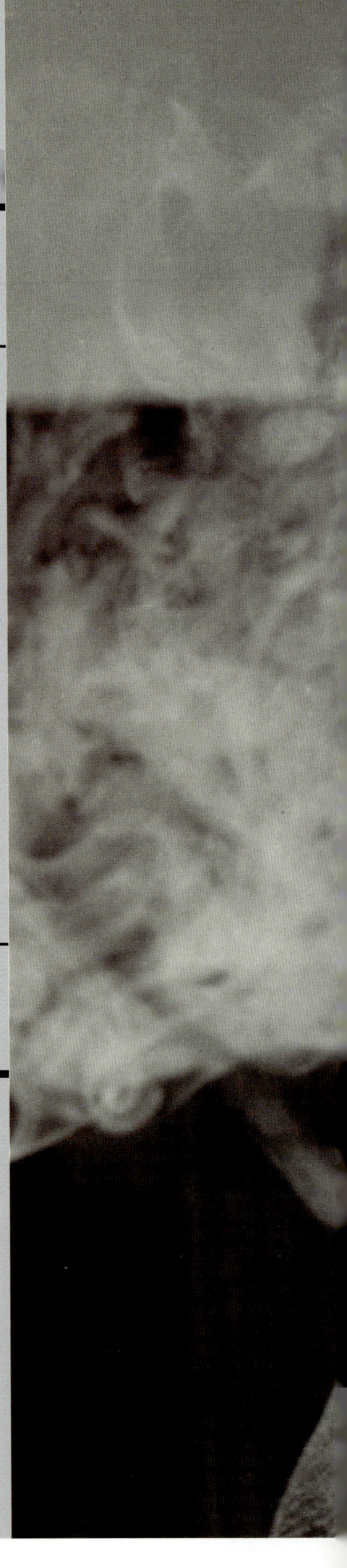

Robinson always went for out and out toerags.

> *If a geezer comes on all 'I respect fuck all' to me, I automatically question whether that includes me.* **DAVE**

Here's a little history lesson for you. In America in 1930 they passed this law in the movie business called the Hays Production Code. I don't know who Hays was but I think if you imagine a bigger nuisance than Mary Whitehouse you'd be on the right lines, cos this geezer's code said this: you are not allowed to glamorize crime or show that crime pays. The only villains we want on the screen are nasty ones. And if they're not nasty, they've got to screw up.

Is it all beginning to make sense now? That's why in Angels With Dirty Faces James Cagney had to get the chair. They could not allow him to survive, cos his character was so likeable. That's why in the original version of Scarface in 1932, they had to add the subtitle The Shame of the Nation just to make sure you understood he was a bad 'un. That's not all. The censors made them tack on this apologetic moral statement to the start of the movie to make sure everyone knew the bad guys had no chance of winning in a decent society and there were loads of extra lines added like 'Don't blame the police – they can't enforce laws that don't exist.' If you look at future films, that's why Heat's ending goes wrong, that's why Al Pacino has to die in the other Scarface, and that's why Goodfellas has him turning grass.

The only good thing to come out of this censorship was Edward G. Robinson. This geezer was another actor, like James Cagney, who pretty much played the same gangster in every film. But where Cagney was the baddy with a heart, Robinson always went for out and out toerags, which meant he could do whatever nasty things he wanted in his films, and cos they showed gangsters as evil pieces of work, the censors were happy to wave them through. Cagney played it like, 'I'm in charge and it's the better of two evils so we'll do this', but Robinson gave us the cigar-smoking bully boy. And Little Caesar, where he plays Rico Bandello, is a blinding example of that.

This geezer is the epitome of the bad baddy. In other words, he is the baddy that the authorities want us to think is normal. There's no good in him at all. He beats up his mum, lies to his mates, kills hostages, throws his weight around and only looks out for number one. He's got no leadership qualities whatsoever, unless you believe that, in order to lead, a boss has to put himself first for the greater good. And if you believe that, there's a flyover somewhere waiting for you to prop it up.

A lot of people think that Rico is the other side of Al Capone. Everyone's got two sides to them, so Cagney played one half of his personality in Angels With Dirty Faces, and here's Robinson giving us the flip version. But that weren't strictly true. He was another one with all the sharp suits, the Crombies, the white silk scarves, the trilbies and the razzmatazz way of doing things, but Rico is more based on a geezer called Salvatore Cardinella, a much more violent and out of control Chicago gangster who was active in the early years of Prohibition. This guy ruled with fear alone, unlike Capone, and that's exactly like Rico, ain't it? When he first gets started in Vettori's gang, he gives it all the 'I ain't afraid of nothin', there's nothin' soft about me, I ain't yella', which the boss likes, but personally I would have had alarm bells going off. If a geezer comes on all 'I respect fuck all' to me, I automatically question whether that includes me. But Vettori doesn't get that, and he pays for it later.

Rico's a selfish little shit. He bullies everyone, even his best mate Joe who actually, I think he had the hots for. Which explains why he has a right fucking downer on women. He goes, 'You go back to that dame and it's suicide. Suicide for both of ya', cos he's thinking of his interests and not Joe's. And there's even a bit of a threat thrown in for good measure.

> **What are the odds on a five-foot Romanian called Emanuel Goldenberg strolling over to Hollywood from Bucharest and becoming one of the world's biggest actors without a Frank Sinatra-type Mafia leg-up?**

Even though he was everything the authorities wanted from their gangsters, it was still easier for the producers to get the film released in 1931 if Rico came to an unpleasant end. It starts when he can't bring himself to shoot his old pal Joe, and from that moment his career as a crime lord is over, cos he's known as soft. So now he's on the run and being taunted by the police chief in the papers every day, and eventually, like a stupid prick, he rises to the bait and gets in touch with the copper. 'This is Rico speaking. Rico! R-I-C-O! Little Caesar, that's who.' You can imagine him shouting that down the phone, can't you, in that classic American gangster voice he had. He was another one with the 'you dirty rat' style and whatever he said sounded scary.

The police track Rico down to a warehouse and he refuses to surrender. Like every stupid boxer out there, he figures he's still got one last fight in him, so he yells, 'If you want me, you'll have to come and get me!' So they do. The police fucking perforate the poster he's hiding behind – it just happens to be advertising Joe's new dance show – and he falls to the floor, all shot up. He's laying there with more holes in him than the Belfry, going, 'Is this the end of Rico?' and the cop standing over him can't believe he didn't stick his hands up when he had the chance. And that's where the Old Bill still go wrong today. Unless you've lived as a criminal, you cannot imagine how a criminal thinks. When you're on the outside of the law, you have more freedom than normal people will ever know, so if it's a choice of life or being banged up where it'll be worse for them than anyone, it's 'Where's my fucking gun?'

If I'm honest, I've known a lot more bad baddies than good ones, and Edward G. Robinson is very realistic in Little Caesar for the era. The gangster world is like any other world and it ain't always 'we look after our own', cos there's too many people in it for them all to be the same. Look at it this way. The reason you'll never get another Al Capone is cos the places they were in charge of were sparse, people-wise, compared to now. The Krays were little Al Capones in the East End. But there was only 15,000 people in the area at the time. Now there's about 250,000. Half of them wouldn't be frightened of two little poofs who own the snooker hall down the road. So you'll never get another period like that.

It's boring but it's all to do with numbers. The reason that the king of Monaco, God bless him, runs such a beautiful country is cos it's so little. It's only got 28 coppers. It's easy to handpick 28 premier division coppers. But because London has got to have 200,000, you're bound to get 50,000 bad ones. I know that cos I used to run 100 doormen. If something happened at one of my clubs and I weren't there, I knew it had to be the other geezer's fault, cos my guy's proper. But when I had 500 doormen it got harder, and half of them I wouldn't have let in my places if they was customers. When you need big numbers, your standards slip. The tests for the police now are a joke because of that: you can be short, four-eyed, ginger and you don't have to be that clever. A GCSE pass, which a sixteen-year-old leaving school could get just by turning up, is the equivalent of the pass needed to get into the force. I sometimes think the police are just trying to embarrass us into going straight, cos it's so pathetic now you can be nicked by a fucking divvy midget. In glasses.

One of the other things Little Caesar had going for it was knowing that Edward G. Robinson probably weren't exactly a stranger to the gangster world anyway. What are the odds on a five-foot Romanian called Emanuel Goldenberg strolling over to Hollywood from Bucharest and becoming one of the world's biggest actors without a little Frank Sinatra-type Mafia leg-up? You've got more chance of getting a wank off a dead Pope, I would have thought. So for that, Mr Robinson, hats off to one of our own.

AND THE MORAL IS...
There are two sides to a coin. For every bloke who robs banks and hurts people just cos it's his job, there's others who do it cos they enjoy it and get a kick out of watching little people squirm. These geezers might help you win a battle, but don't show them your back when they're washing up the carving knives.

Don Corleone
by Marlon Brando

FACTS

**MARLON BRANDO
THE GODFATHER (1972)
THE GODFATHER II (1974)**

DAVE'S FILM FACTS

Directed by Francis Ford Coppola. Screenplays by Mario Puzo and Francis Ford Coppola. Two of the most influential gangster movies of all time, The Godfather I and II show how much the great American families really are only families. Everything is kept in house, you don't line up with outsiders and, above all, it's only business. Marlon Brando as ageing gang boss Don Corleone, his heir Michael (Al Pacino) and hothead elder son Sonny (James Caan) absolutely made the roles of post-war gangsters their own. Even 1990's Godfather III, although shit compared to the first two, opened your eyes to how the top families have so much money and influence they have as many kosher businesses as bent ones. And they're often the most 'honest' geezers around the boardroom table.

ANYTHING YOU SAY WILL BE TAKEN DOWN…

'I made him an offer he couldn't refuse.'

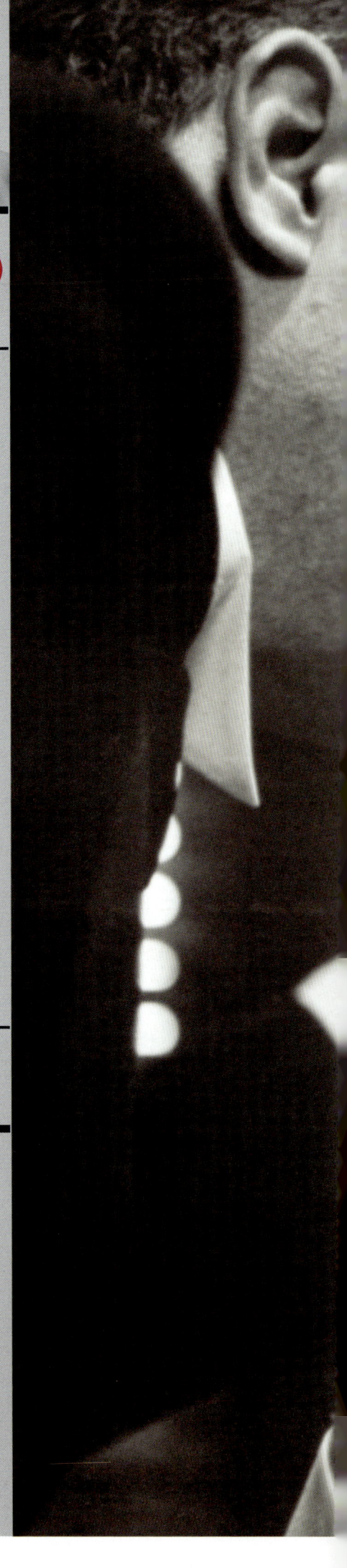

DAVE'S DUSTER-O-METER
INFLUENCE 5
LEADERSHIP 5
SUCCESS 5
NAUGHTINESS 5
AUTHENTICITY 5

Even if you don't think you know any other gangster movies (and if you don't, what the fuck are you doing reading this book?), everyone's heard of The Godfather. It's been spoofed by every comedian who's ever lived, they sell ravioli on the telly using a guy dressed as Marlon Brando, and it's got the most famous line from a villain in cinema history. Altogether now: 'I made him an offer he couldn't refuse.'

How fucking sinister is that? He don't say, 'I put a gun to his head and threatened to empty his brains over the shagpile' or 'After eight hours of being Breville toasted he decided to talk.' There's no detail, no description of what happened, and that's what sends shivers up you. That's when you know you're in the company of the real deal. It's the two-bit gobshite who has to lay on all the gory details to make people scared of him and respect him. A genuine premier division hardman does not need to boast: all he says is he made the geezer an 'offer' and – guess what? – that geezer accepted.

What makes it proper classy is this. When you hear the phrase for the first time, Al Pacino's character Michael Corleone lets you in on the full story about how his dad, Vito Corleone, had actually tried to do the right thing. This Glenn Miller-type bandleader is offered $10,000 to let Don Corleone's godson, Johnny Fontane, out of his contract with his band. The punk says no. So Brando pops back with one of his boys, Luca Brasi, who, in case you've never met him, is one right scary fuck. Brasi holds a gun to the bandleader's head and Brando says either his signature or his brains is going on the contract. Refuse that, prick.

See what I mean about class? He didn't just steam in with the boys, he gave the cunt a chance to do the right thing and make a bit of cash in the process. But some people have got to learn to take a hint.

The next time Vito Corleone says he's gonna make someone an offer he can't refuse, everyone on the planet knows what happens next. Grans know it, kids know it, blokes who've spent 27 years in solitary on Robben Island know it. Even Shergar fans know it: Vegas hotel scheister Moe Green wakes up with the head of his champion thoroughbred Khartoum in bed next to him. Talk about a photo finish.

Everyone raves about that scene, and rightly so, especially in this country. Over here, you might get the odd serial killer who leaves a little trinket or something at the scene of the crime, but that's about it. It's Americans who go in for all the theatrical stuff, all the big gestures and that element of razzmatazz, even when it comes to killing.

I can understand all that, cos I myself am very theatrical. I'll give you an example. Other people might carry a knuckleduster, but who else's is 18-carat gold with diamonds embedded in it? My duster is actually worth 27 grand. That is to say, the tiara that it used to be was worth that much. But I'd have looked a right cunt in a tiara so when the item came into my, er, possession, I had it melted down into this beauty. The only trouble is, if I proper connect with a geezer's chin, it has been known for the odd diamond to work its way out and get embedded among the stubble. You look a right prick kneeling over a bloke with a hole in his jaw going, 'Hold still, mate, there's still one in your beard.'

But because I'm a bit more on their wavelength, if you like, when I see the scene with the famous Mr 'Ead laying there, I probably have a different take on it to a lot of people. If you watch it and go, 'What a great scene in a great film. That's scary. Who'd have thought of that?' then that's great and the director's done a top job. But I watch it and it's a bit different, cos I can see where the gangsters are coming from. To me that scene

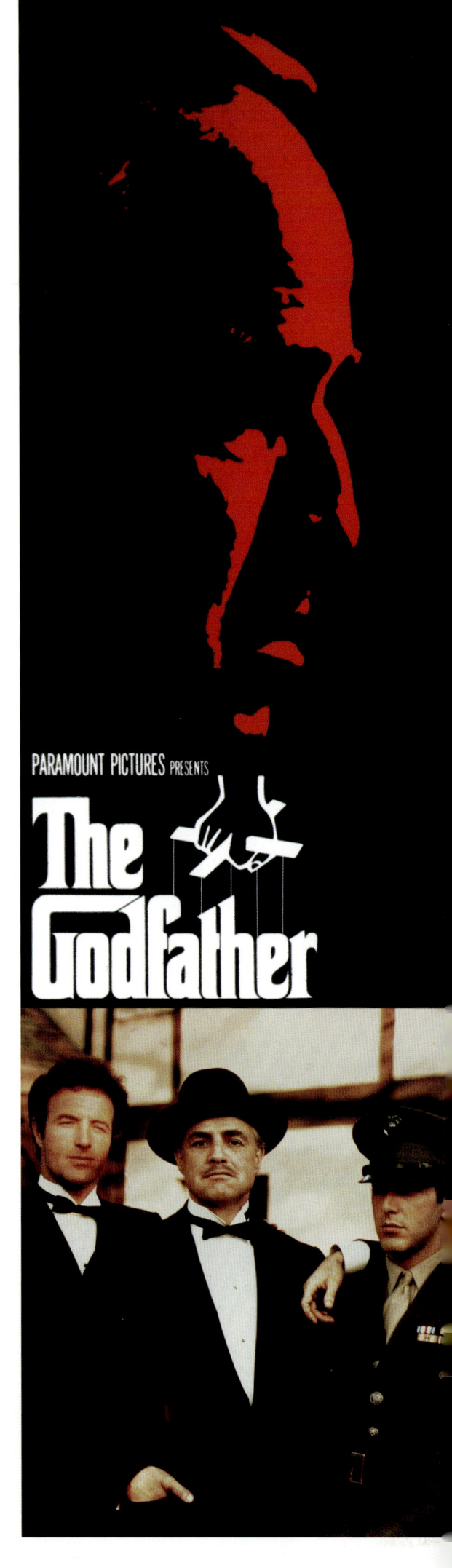

The next time Pacino says he's gonna make someone an offer he can't refuse, everyone on the planet knows what happens next. Grans know it, kids know it, blokes who've spent 27 years in solitary on Robben Island know it.

says, 'If I can chop the head off a horse, which is hard cos it's three ton, and then get it upstairs and in your bed while you're asleep, what the fuck could I do to you or your kids or your wife if I wanted to?' That's really where that one runs deep for me.

I'll tell you something else that rings a few bells with me. When the film kicks off, old man Brando is sitting in his lounge receiving all these guests. It's like your average day at Cynthia Payne's, cos they're pouring in, all these geezers after a favour from the proud father on the day of his daughter's wedding. That might be a fuck-off fantastic scene to show his power an' that, but it's absolutely true to life. Scale it down, and that's what happens in my house on a daily basis.

Every little pocket of naughty boys has a pecking order and my place in it has always been this: I might not be the greatest fighter, but I know a man who is and I've probably employed him. When I was active, I was known as 'The Yellow Pages of Crime' because my greatest talent is for putting the right people with the right jobs. Whether you've got a leaky tap, a noisy neighbour or a squashed paddy has turned up under your wheel arch, one call can sort you out. Forget the AA, I'm like the fourth emergency service. There's the Old Bill, Fireman Sam, the Casualty mob, and then there's Dave. It's like that old Mr T thing, ain't it? If you've got a problem and no one else can help you, and if you can find them, maybe you can hire The A-Team. Well, I'm fucking easy to find. I live in a white castle with a 40-foot picture of me on the side. Come on down.

So I get loads of visitors, and the majority of them are just normal people: bakers, mechanics, even other fucking authors. But cos my house is all CCTV'd up by the authorities, all the copper across the road filming it sees is just a load of geezers coming in in Crombies and hats. One day they'll use all this film in court and go, 'On this day 37 darkly dressed men entered his house for reasons unknown.' That's why I always tell my guests to give the cameras a wave on their way out.

Before he corks it in his vineyard and hands the reins over to Pacino, Brando is the epitome of perfect leader material. A real boss should be someone who's unexcitable, who doesn't make decisions to impress anyone else, and who would rather risk a bit of egg on his face than gamble his boys' lives on settling a score they might not win. The art of disguise is the most important thing about any boss, and I don't mean stuffing cotton wool in your mouth like Brando did, neither. At one point he says to Pacino, 'Never let anyone outside the family know what you're thinking' and that information is priceless. Being able to not let on whether you've got the hump or you ain't, or whether you're shitting a brick or you're cool as ice, could save your life. At the very least it will piss your enemies off cos they don't know what you're up to, and that's always worth buying a ticket for.

Brando also demonstrates the art of being honest without upsetting people, which is another leader quality that isn't in too full supply. But the main thing he has going for him when the film starts is his age. Just reaching old age in this business deserves a clap, but having got there, what you've learned on the way is amazing. There's no substitute for experience and again, when you've seen it all before, it's one of them things that can save a lot of lives. When you're 70 and a situation crops up, it's like flicking through a reference book in your head, cos you go, 'Well, what happens here normally? Ah yeah, it'll probably kick off like that so we'll do this…'

So he is able to pass on knowledge without being looked at as bossy and when violence and punishment is being dished out, he makes it very, very, very thorough and very professional. So even if the act was bad – and to be honest, some countries do view murder

Other people might carry a knuckleduster, but who else's is 18-carat gold with diamonds embedded in it? My duster is actually worth 27 grand. **DAVE**

as quite bad – it was so nicely done you had to go, 'Ooh. Round of applause.' He makes it very clear why something's happening, so no one thinks he's out of control. Everyone knows the rules and what will happen to them if they step out of line.

And that's why his boy Santino is such a shit choice as Godfather and Michael's the bollocks. None of Brando's decisions are made in anger or in a hurry – even when he's been shot, he goes to the meeting with the other bosses and guarantees there'll be no revenge from him as long as his family aren't harmed. Which ain't exactly Sonny's style. Apart from a bridesmaid he bangs who gets a full one, everything else he does is half-cocked. He tries to hit his brother-in-law for a home run for smacking his sister, and gets himself killed by running into a trap at full speed without working it out first.

That's a fucking scene and a half, ain't it? Next time you're slowing down to chuck a quid in the automatic booths at Dartford Tunnel, imagine twenty geezers with Uzis popping up and turning your motor into Swiss cheese. But talk about realistic – that sort of thing happens in America, it really does. We might not hear about it though, for the very simple reason the authorities don't want us to idolize that sort of behaviour. Keep in mind we're a little island, with an island mentality, so it's easy for them to keep that sort of thing off our news, cos they don't want us going, 'Yeah, that's how to take care of your enemies.' Cos we copy the Yanks on everything else – taking the laces out of trainers, wearing hats back to front, trousers hanging down to our bollocks – they know we would have some macabre interest in a scene like that and before you know it they'd have a few copycats on the M6 toll road. But pound for pound, you get more nutters over there than you do over here so it does happen.

One of the reasons the police try to shut me down is cos they spend millions of pounds on plod PR trying to convince the country that crime don't pay, and there's me making it look like a fucking career option. But for anyone who is considering entering the profession, this film should be compulsory viewing. Take the scene where Michael blows away the other gang boss and the Chief of Police. Any cunt thinks he could shoot someone for the first time, but the Godfather's boys make sure Michael's clued up on every single detail before he goes in so he can just switch to autopilot and get through it. Otherwise you might pop a guy and be freaked and go, 'Fuck, where's all this blood coming from? The puddle's getting bigger and bigger – it's gonna reach me!' You might be standing there panting like Lassie on heat for a minute and a half, just looking at it, which is more than enough time for everyone else to get up from hiding under their tables and begin to use your brain for target practice.

But if you know what I know, you realize you've got half a chance of getting away with it. I assure you from experience that if you go into a crowded place and stick a shot in the air, everyone hits the floor and stays there for at least five seconds. And I mean everyone. Even if you're only doing it to make your wife do it, you will still hit the deck. So you could stroll into a restaurant, let one off in the air and do what the fuck you like unchallenged for the next few seconds, cos there'll be no fucker interested in you. I guarantee that, cos I've been there, done that and got the carpet burns to prove it.

So if you've never shot anyone before, which Michael hadn't, you need to be told about the hyperventilating (that you'll get) or the twitching (that's the other geezer). You're going, 'I've plugged him ten times and he's still fucking moving!' so you have to talk someone through every stage of it. It's like when I go to court. You get your story straight in your head, you practise it on everyone, then when you get up into the dock, you're straight in on auto-chat. You sound so fucking convincing, even you think you're telling the truth.

A real boss would be someone who's unexcitable, who doesn't make decisions to impress anyone else.

I'll tell you something else that I know happens in real life, cos I experienced it. When Brando's been shot and Pacino turns up at the hospital and finds his bed unguarded, that's perfectly realistic. Exactly the same thing happened to me after my crash a few years ago. I was unconscious when I arrived at the hospital and my boys didn't know what had happened. The whisper was it was a gangland hit, and that was close enough although it was actually the police who tried to kill me. (It's all there in my book Fuck the Ride.) As soon as they learn that, the last thing my boys want is a policeman guarding my room, what with all them life-support leads just dangling there begging to be accidentally pulled out. So from the moment I was wheeled in in bits until I came out six months later, they made sure I had the sort of 24-hour security only flat-nosed, bald-headed chaps can give you. It made it a bit awkward when a new doctor come round – 'your name's not on the list, mate, so you're not going in' – but I probably owe them my life.

Because other people see me as a bit of a Godfather figure, although I'd never put myself in the same bracket personally, I can see similarities between my life and what Don Corleone was trying to do with his. The reason he falls out with the rest of the gangs is cos he won't touch drugs. For me, the world of the old-fashioned criminal ended when the narcotics business started to take over. Honour amongst thieves, respect and all them other qualities that villains could take a bit of heart from, they all fucked out the window the moment people started doing deals worth £20 million instead of 20 grand and multicultural elements got involved.

The other thing he was ahead of his time on, and which I still do to this day, is keeping a foothold in the legitimate world. He had all these judges and senators in his back pocket, and I've had more bent coppers on my books than covers. Bribes will only get you so far, though, so the real high flyers in the criminal

fraternity, like in any business, will have the best lawyers. But it's no good having the best if he don't answer his phone cos he's reading up on another case; you actually want him to love you and be thinking about you all the time. And the way to achieve it is this: family.

The Godfather has his adopted son Tom Hagen as his brief, and that's what all the main players do these days. All the big Russian crime families are putting their sons through Oxford, Eton and all that but under a different name to them, so he comes out at the end of it a High Court lawyer. Then they find a top firm and say, 'I want you to employ my son for a year, and here's the money to pay him', just so he can have that on his CV. Job done. The higher up the ladder you get the more important a good solicitor is. And I used to have a fantastic one, Ralph Haeems. He was the barrister for the Krays – not that that's a great advert, they got 30 fucking years!

AND THE MORAL IS...
Step outside the family and you'll be swimming with the fishes. When Michael says, 'Fredo, you're my brother and I love you, but don't ever take sides with anyone against the family again', you know it's not an idle threat. Killing your own brother is the hardest order to give in the world, but Michael does it coolly and clinically for the good of the family.

Tony Montana
by Al Pacino

FACTS

AL PACINO SCARFACE (1983)

DAVE'S FILM FACTS

Directed by Brian De Palma. Screenplay by Oliver Stone. Taking its name from Howard Hawks' 1932 film based on Al Capone, Scarface was written by Oliver Stone and stars Al Pacino as drug baron Tony Montana who arrives in Florida as one of the thousands of Cubans taking advantage of the opening of the port at Mariel Harbour. Famed for its violence (42 deaths) and bad language (182 'fucks') the film was originally refused a cinema rating. It was also the movie that made Michelle Pfeiffer a star.

ANYTHING YOU SAY WILL BE TAKEN DOWN…

'Say hello to my little friend.'

There ain't a young villain alive who can't identify with Scarface. This is their film. In fact, Al Pacino's character probably secretly has every criminal's admiration because of the theatrical way that he dies. I know if I was in that position, I'd want to go out like that. You don't even mind him dying because you're going, 'Yes!' at the way he does it.

And what a great line that is: 'Say hello to my little friend!' However non-violent and patient you are, everyone has got a limit, somewhere where you would actually go, 'Fuck that!' And that little scene there where you go, 'You fucking arseholes, have that!' is the epitome of it. It's a premier division testosterone scene and you really think he can take on an army. I have a wank every time I watch that!

The black and white film from 1932 that this is based on is highly rated by a lot of people because of the way it deals with Al Capone's life in Chicago. To be honest, that's a little bit before my time, but there's nothing in this version that I haven't seen with my own eyes, so the Tony Montana story is the one for me.

I actually know a Tony Montana. He's a black, American professional party man who lives in the West End. Funny as fuck, and he's got the longest tongue I've ever seen. If you go, 'Show us, Tony', he rolls it up inside his mouth then just unfurls it down to the bottom of his neck like red carpet being unrolled down his face. What the fuck is that? You know ox tongue that you can buy in the butcher's? It's like that. Fucking mental.

But the other Tony Montana is all about the American Dream, ain't he? Start from the bottom, get right to the top, that's the way. That's not just the American Dream, though, that's the Peckham Dream, it's every fucker's dream, wherever you're from. Who wouldn't want all them trappings? Obviously the world of the premier division drug dealer is not something I come into contact with regularly,

> **Start from the bottom, get right to the top, that's the way. That's not American Dream, though, it's the Peckham Dream**

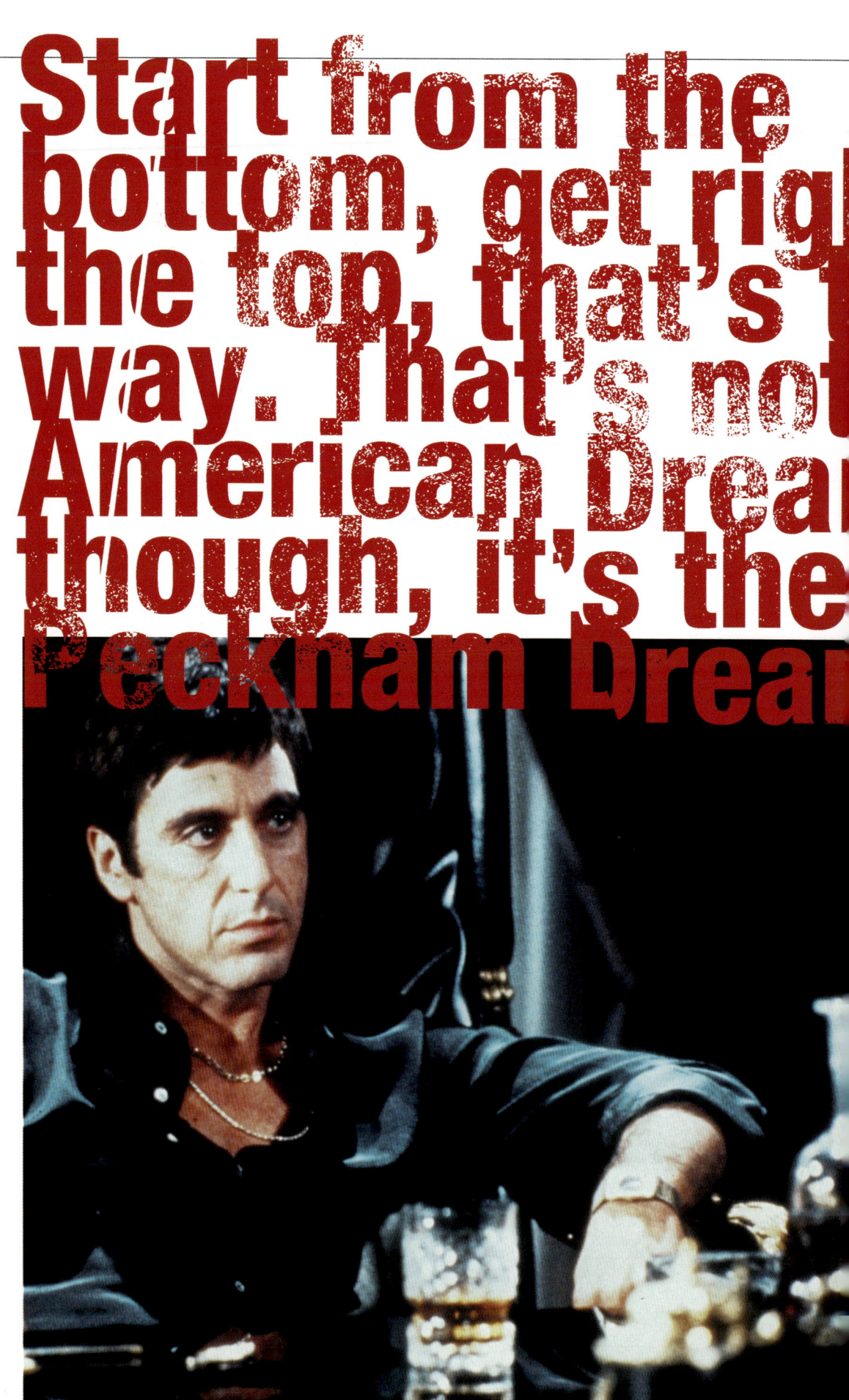

> 'You make the money first. Then when you get the money, you get the power. Then when you get the power, you get the women.' **DAVE**

pulls that I have actually employed regularly in my own life. You remember when he goes to see his boss after the night club shooting has gone tits up, and he gets his mate to ring his boss while he was there to say it all went wrong? Well I do that all the time. I get people to ring the person I'm with and say something that I have prepared, because I want to see the geezer's instant reaction first hand. So I know what the voice has said on the phone, I've seen the guy in front of me react, and now I want to know what he's going to say to me. Whether he knows it or not, I'm holding all the fucking aces and he's the weakest link. Goodbye, cunt.

For all the glamorous lifestyle bit, though, the actual day-to-day business of an international drug dealer isn't anything to get hard over. It might be a very graphic word that has strong criminal images, but a 'drug dealer' is basically just a salesman. He certainly ain't a gangster. A gangster is the guy who says, 'You dirty rat', 'Stick 'em up' and all that. A drug dealer might as well be selling fucking Tupperware door to door. He's on the phone saying, 'I've got these cheap lunchboxes, do you know anyone who wants them?' Well, if he knows the geezer in Taiwan who makes them and another geezer who sells them at Hamley's, he can make a lot of money. Just like that, it's all fell in his hat. And drug dealers don't do much more than that. They pick up the phone and ask you if you want to buy something, then you go round and pick it up. It's telesales.

But because they sell and buy from people who would be deemed criminal, they start to think that they themselves are gangsters. So suddenly you're not happy with just being a salesman, you want to be a salesman with a gun.

And that's where the trouble starts, once you start trying to do something you're not good at. If you're a burglar, you're not a fucking tough guy so why have you got that knife in your back pocket? You climb in windows and nick stereos, you're not a hard nut. And if you are a hard nut, don't pretend you're a go-getter bank robber, cos you're not, you're just a good fighter. One man, one job. You might be able to have a proper tear up but you haven't got a brain cell in your head. Horses for courses.

So Tony Montana was a good wheeler and dealer who got so successful he ended up running his own empire. He weren't no Winston Churchill, he weren't no leader of men and he weren't no hitman. The problem he had was the higher up you go in the criminal world, the bigger weapon you need. Whether you want it or not, if the people you're in competition with have serious weapons, you need to have them if only to keep them at arm's length. Cos if they thought that if they come to your house and shot you they could have all your Charlie, they would do it. Just like that, that's what the drugs trade is like. So you need to be seen to be tooled up to protect yourself and your business. Fight fire with fucking fire.

The other problem Montana has that affects people in real life is the more successful he becomes, the more out of touch with normal people he gets. I've met a few players like that, who have been proper turned by what the money and the power can let them get away with.

Look at it this way: even if you're a good fighter, why waste your time and effort clumping some twat when you can pay someone to do it for you? Or even better, if you meet someone who would shoot someone else for you and it would cost you next to nothing, the next time you had an argument you wouldn't even think about bashing the guy up. You don't have to mess your nice suit up, waste twenty seconds on the floor and walk away panting like a dog with all snot hanging off your nose, cos you know you could ring this little Kosovan to turn up and shoot the cunt. It's that easy and when you've done it once you never want to have another dust-up again. Why would

> *I've got people around me that are loose cannons, but I keep them as my friends.* **DAVE**

you when you could just pick up the phone and let your fingers do the fighting?

The rise of the drugs trade and the silly money behind it has killed off any idea of respect in the gangster fraternity in real life, which is why you get things like that and death sentences dished out for fuck all. But in Scarface Tony's basically a good kid from the old school 'honour amongst thieves' tradition. He's all, 'I never fucked anybody over in my life that didn't have it coming to them' – and that's the way the best of us are. All he's got in the world is his word and his balls, and he ain't in a rush to break either of them for anyone.

Before he goes off the cake, he's proper clued up on how things work in America. 'You make the money first. Then when you get the money, you get the power. Then when you get the power, you get the women.' What he don't say is, when you get the drugs, you get more so-called friends than you can count – and this is a geezer who works in millions so he knows some pretty big numbers.

Any sense of proportion goes right out the fucking window when drugs come in, even if you're just a user. Because cocaine is such a sociable drug, a 50-quid gram will always set you back 100 nicker, cos you always end up buying twice as much as you want. It works like this: you never go in the toilets on your own to do a line, do you? It's got that stigma – 'What? You sneaked off and had a line by yourself, you slippery little cunt?' So you always say to your mate, 'You want to do some?' And that means, in order to have a full gram of Charlie yourself, you've got to buy another one for your mates.

Once you're in a position where you're dealing it and you've got tons of it around, and everyone knows you have, then it's a million billion times worse. Suddenly you're Mr Popular, not cos you're a nice guy but because you're always offering gear. Every time someone comes round, you go, 'Want a line?' It's sociable, it's nice. And you do lines that you could mark the fucking road with, you know what I mean? They're so big you could put cat's eyes in them. And that's why they're visiting you.

And because your friends have a line, you end up doing one, so you're always out your head. And then the shit starts to hit. You're forced into predicaments where you start thinking it's real life. In your head you really are a popular guy and all these people like you and genuinely want you to come to all their parties and – wow – all these girls all want to fuck you.

But that's not gonna hurt you. What really fucks you up is when you start making decisions on the gear like he does. Any decision made in anger is probably gonna be wrong, that's rule number one. But that's nothing like trying to do things when you're out your fucking head. The problem with Charlie is you think you're all right but you're really just mugging yourself off. And what happens is, because you're in charge, no one tells you you're coming out with a load of bollocks. Everyone comes to you for fucking advice, they don't expect you to need it. Outsiders can see you walking into a fucking problem better than you can, but they think, 'It's Dave Courtney – he must know what he's fucking doing.' So I walk in and get shot, or killed or – worse – nicked, and then they go, 'Well, I knew that was gonna happen.' 'So why didn't you tell me?' 'Cos you're Dave Courtney.' The only time Tony Montana gets any straight talking is when he's a nobody.

What makes him a proper dozy cunt, though, is the fact that he thinks he can handle the Charlie even though he can see what it's doing to all his mates and in particular to his missus. Michelle Pfeiffer was perfectly cast as Elvira, weren't she? You know, beautiful, smart, with all the trappings of the coke-dealing villain. And fucking good wanking material an' all. In actual fact, she is exactly what you don't need if you're a gangster – in reality, the professional, successful naughtyman has to have an anchor, not some stupid eighteen-year-old who just distracts him and shags his mates. The phrase 'gangsters' moll' is a bit of a media invention, to be honest, but that doesn't mean they're not out there. I'm just saying, it's never gonna end pretty with someone like that.

Even before the Charlie gets its grip, Montana is paranoid and ever so slightly violent. South American and Mediterranean people are like that, it's in their make-up, and I don't mean their lipstick. Their genes are different, they're a bit more fucking hyper. You see them all on the hooters of the cars, right fucking sweating and bug-eyed, screaming in each other's faces at a thousand miles an hour – and they're only asking for a fag. And cos they're like this, if there's anything in their hands when they're arguing, they'll use it.

There are also a lot of 'Tony Montana' figures out there. My advice to anyone who knows one is to befriend him cos he likes to be liked. You know that saying: keep your friends close but your enemies closer? Remember it, it could save your life. I've got people around me that are loose cannons but I keep them as my friends because I don't want them to be anyone else's, cos they're off the wall. Every time they come out with me as my mate I'm shitting myself in case they punch someone in the head. But I'd rather run that risk than fall out with their other mate and have them on my back.

Tony Montana isn't really a bad man, that's why you befriend him. The only people he's violent to in his little cut-throat world are people that deserve it. And the only people he fucked are the people who tried to fuck him first.

AND THE MORAL IS...
Every time Tony Montana made a bad decision he was out of his head. When he shot his sister's husband, he was out of his head. When he bashed the geezer up in the toilet he was out of his head. Don't get high on your own supply.

Henry Hill
by Ray Liotta

FACTS
RAY LIOTTA GOODFELLAS (1990)

DAVE'S FILM FACTS
Directed by Martin Scorsese. Screenplay by Nicholas Pileggi and Martin Scorsese. The true story of gangster turned federal informant Henry Hill. From wide-eyed kid to street wise-guy, Goodfellas tells of his ascendancy into the New York mafia, aided and abetted by partners in crime Jimmy Conway (Robert De Niro) and Tommy DeVito (Joe Pesci). Scorsese's choice of a pop music soundtrack over some of the most gruesome scenes in cinema history made the images even more shocking.

ANYTHING YOU SAY WILL BE TAKEN DOWN…
'How am I funny, like a clown? What is so funny about me? What the fuck is funny about me? Tell me. Tell me what's funny.'

Before it [went] sour, Goo[dfellas was] like a docu[mentary] in ho[w] gangste[rs...] how reali[stic...]

> *Anyone who sells out his mates to save his own skin ain't really worth glorifying in my opinion.* **DAVE**

goodfellas is all documentary to me. to be a gangster. That's just stic it is.

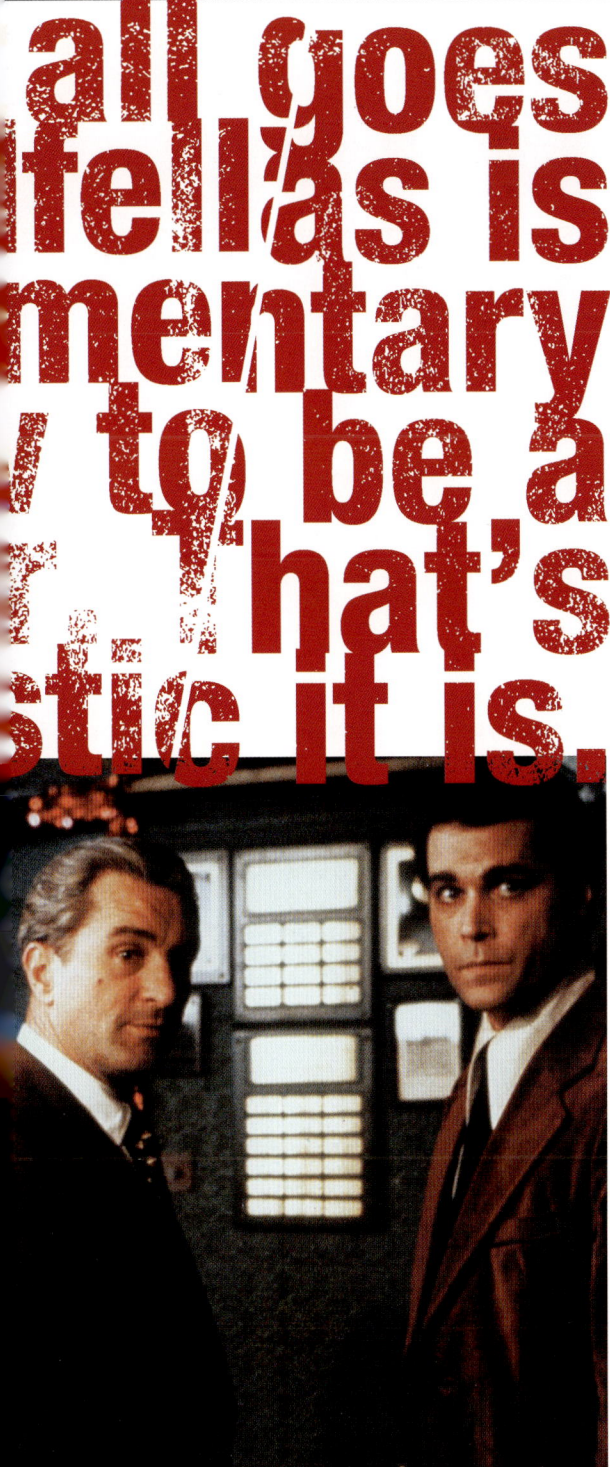

Ninety-five per cent of people won't have heard of Henry Hill, but you've all heard of Goodfellas, which is his story.

It's a great film and all that, and Martin Scorsese has proper done the business this time, but, from a criminal's point of view, what made it a classic in my eyes was it showed why people want to be a villain in the first place. Remember that line: 'As far back as I can remember, I've always wanted to be a gangster.' That, for me, is what the whole movie is about.

The scene with Henry as a little boy with 'wow' in his eyes, just looking and wanting to grow up into one of the wise-guys outside his window with the hot wheels and the even hotter chicks – that explains everything you need to know about why anyone gets started in this business. It was the perfect advert for why some people turn out like that. You could seriously go, 'Look at that film, Mum and Dad. That's what happened to me. That's how romantic I found it, that's how I got suckered into it, that's how I got trapped in it when I wanted to get out, that's why I ended up going with her.' It's not that easy for a grown man, especially a villain, to go, 'I just found it all glittery and nice.' It's easier to go, 'Yeah, I just am a gangster, all right?' But Goodfellas explained everything that people genuinely do find hard to tell others if you're in that way of life.

It also paints a fucking scarily real picture of the life of the gangster's wife. When they're courting, Ray Liotta's Henry takes his bird Karen to see a show at the Copacabana club. She thinks it's a bit odd when he walks her past the queues out the front and down an alley into a service entrance. They go through the kitchens, round the staff corridors, past the security boys and the off-duty waiters, and out into the main area. They get to the front and these geezers appear and literally lift a table and chairs over to them to sit at. How impressive is that? Suddenly they're in the front row and she realizes her bloke's not all he seems.

When they get married and she's in the thick of his life, Karen discovers what all gangsters' wives discover soon enough: that they can't have friends outside the 'family' no more. It's just not safe. And that's fucking lonely when you're not expecting it. Imagine you go to pick up the kids from school and all the other mums are gassing about what they've been up to. What can Henry Hill's missus say? 'You'll never guess what? My Henry brought home this dead geezer hanging with the cows in an abattoir lorry the other day. A right fucking laugh that was.' My missus Jennifer went through that on a daily basis. Yes, I was a complete wanker and I showed off to the hilt with all the 'Don't worry about queuing, Mr Courtney, this one's on us' and 'Your usual table, Mr Courtney?' But day to day it's an us and them situation, and for the bird it's worse cos they never signed up for all that. They just wanted to be with you, and because of that they get cut off from the outside world.

I know Henry Hill's the star, cos it was based on his book, and Ray Liotta's got that sort of gangster down to a T, but cos I've made a film myself I'm not that impressed by all the 'it's a true story' shit. In Hollywood, all 'true story' means is it's as true as he wants us to believe. What happens is you hear one bloke's good story, that bloke's good story, that bloke's good story and another one's, and put them all together in one big story with bits of your own. His one might have happened in Brazil, his happened in Ireland, his happened upstairs in his mum's house and his one he just heard from some bloke in prison, but now, cos you're telling it, they're all happening in the Bronx.

My main problem with Hill, though, is no one likes a grass. Especially the bloke on the other end of the information. Anyone who sells out his mates to save his own skin ain't really worth glorifying in my opinion, which is what

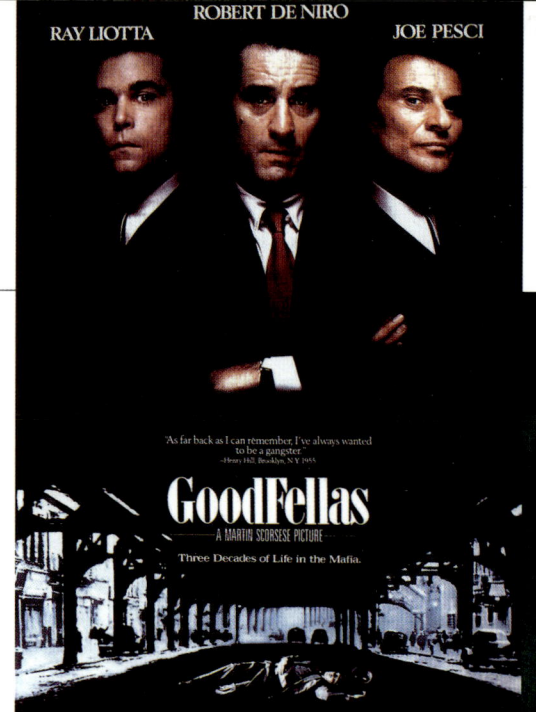

ruins the film for me. And when you think that in all his interviews, Henry Hill tells you what a main player he is, but in the film he's a supposedly innocent bystander while his mates do all the dirty work – shut the fuck up! He's either lied in real life or he's lied in the film. Either way that makes him lower than a snake's arsehole.

So the ending totally ruined the whole thing for me, but it is horribly realistic. Even though it's a true story, I would rather it finished that he died or got caught and went to prison, than portrayed as a grass to the criminal fraternity. To me, it's a geezer strung out on Charlie getting so paranoid that when he's actually describing what's happening to him he can actually make you believe his own mates are turning on him, and he's got to grass them up for the good. In reality, they weren't going to do fuck all to him cos he was doing it behind their backs. But other people could watch the film and go, 'Gangsters are all dirty cunts and the authorities have to win.' But actually as a gangster it makes you go, 'We're not like that!'

But before it all goes sour, Goodfellas is like a documentary in how to be a gangster. That's how realistic it is. I know loads of Robert De Niro characters, loads of geezers just in it for the rush of putting together a job and getting away with it. He ain't in it that long, but old Bobby don't disappoint as usual. He's the one who tells Hill, 'Never rat on your friends and always keep your mouth shut', although fuck lot of good that did him. And he's the one who tries to get him away from the grip of Frosty the Snowman. He's leader material, without a shadow of a doubt.

But it's Joe Pesci as Tommy DeVito that we all remember, ain't it? I'm not saying that's who we all want to be like, cos fuck me that type's trouble. But watching him going through all that 'you think I'm funny?' nutter schtick you know you're in for some top drawer entertainment.

I know from experience there's more Joe Pescis around than Robert De Niros. That's a real character. I've got two or three of them. They're the ones I say you have to keep on board, knowing they're going to be a fucking tinderbox when you're out. But the alternative to not being his mate is being his enemy. You don't want any of that cos once he's thrown his hat in someone else's ring, it's to the end as far as he's concerned. Where someone else might try and plan something clever, he'd just run over to your house and shoot you and worry about it later. Everyone knows a Joe Pesci, and their actions end up being spread out where the rewards are concerned, and always eventually come back to me. He does something wrong and it's, 'Courtney's firm have just come in here and stabbed some geezer in the eye with a pen.' But that weren't me!

It's like the geezer he plays in Casino but even more off the cake. He's one of those typical Mediterranean nutty boys, who always sound like you've just pissed on their nan even if they just want to know the time.

The higher up in the gangster world you go, the more of a liability that type of person is. If someone annoys them on the street, where once they'd have given them a slap, now, cos they've got guns in their pockets, they pop one in his head. Most full-blooded eye-contact confrontations end up with one of you dying, cos you both know that if it don't get finished there and then, the other one's gonna be walking away thinking, 'I'll have you, you cunt' and so it's better to act now than spend the next few days looking over your shoulder.

The thing is, like with any crime, as soon as you've done that once in real life, it ain't so scary any more and you think you can get away with it all the time.

The thing is, like with any crime, as soon as you've done that once in real life, it ain't so scary any more and you think you can get away with it all the time. That's why Ronnie and Reggie Kray thought they could walk into a pub and go 'bang' and get away with it. Cos they had done it before. But it's true and I see it happening. Once you do something and get , away with it, it's almost like you start to think it's legal. The first time you sell drugs in a club you're frightened someone's gonna catch you. After a week of doing it you realize no one minds, so you don't hide in the toilets all night. After three weeks you're paying the doorman to let you know if there's any customers in, and after eight weeks you might as well have a stall going 'Es, trips, grass and whizz a pound!' You forget it's not legal till you're driving home and someone goes, 'You're nicked.'

AND THE MORAL IS...
Keep your loose cannons under observation at all times. It's good to have a hothead in your firm, but you've got to be prepared to clean up after them. And that don't mean turning state's evidence, prick.

Neil McCauley
by Robert De Niro

FACTS
ROBERT DE NIRO
HEAT (1995)

DAVE'S FILM FACTS
Written and Directed by Michael Mann. Robert De Niro plays super-smooth thief and gang boss Neil McCauley. Al Pacino is the hard-bitten cop Vincent Hanna obsessed with tracking McCauley down. Despite both appearing in Godfather II, Heat is the first time Pacino and De Niro have acted together. Co-stars include Val Kilmer, Natalie Portman, John Voight and Ashley Judd. Mann based the movie on a cop friend in Chicago who dedicated his career to bring down one villain.

ANYTHING YOU SAY WILL BE TAKEN DOWN…

Vincent Hanna:
I don't know how to do anything else.

Neil McCauley:
Neither do I.

Vincent Hanna:
I don't much want to either.

Neil McCauley:
Neither do I.

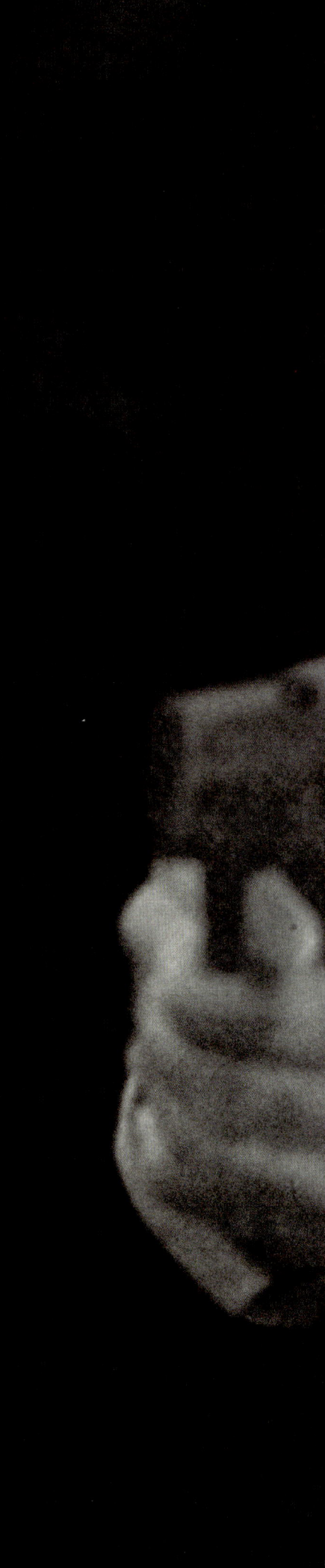

This is a geezer who lives, breathes, drinks and screws his job. And that's realistic.

> *You can't afford to let anything get in the way of business, whichever side you're on.* **DAVE**

Without any shadow of a doubt, the criminals' criminal film and the gangsters' gangster movie is this one: Heat. I don't know how anyone else judges a film – and considering this is my list I don't really give a shit – but as far as meaning something to real-life villains, and actually doing things on screen that happen every day to authentic naughty boys, Heat's pretty much the bollocks.

The thing about this one that sets it apart, though, is the copper. Robert De Niro plays a blinding heist merchant, Neil McCauley, and you've got to respect him. Top drawer job as usual. But you've also got Al Pacino as this chewed up lieutenant Vincent Hanna tracking him down, and as far as reality goes, he's got that part nailed down.

This is a guy with a drink problem, a wife problem, a daughter problem, a fucking dandruff problem, trouble with his car, bad breath and he can't sleep – anything you can think of, he's got it. And imagine coming home to that? His current wife gives him grief for bringing his corpses to bed with him, which I hope she don't mean literally, but you get the idea. This is a geezer who lives, breathes, drinks and screws his job. And that's realistic. As a profession, policemen have the highest divorce rate in the country cos of the pressures of the work. (That, of course, and the fact they're all wankers.)

There are lots of standout scenes in Heat, and a load of people will tell you the airfield chase bit is the nuts, but that didn't do it for me. From where I'm sitting you will not get a better idea of reality from Hollywood than when Pacino pulls De Niro over at the side of the road. He's been chasing him for years and getting nowhere, so he goes, 'Fuck this,' sticks his blue lights on and stops De Niro's car. Then he goes up to him and says, 'Hello, fancy a drink?' This is where it gets interesting, cos there are coppers that would actually do that and villains who would actually take them up on it and go, 'Yes, I'll have a drink with you.' There are also some who'd go, 'Fuck you' and I've done both. I like to do things to mess with the Old Bill and catch them out on purpose, so I'm looking at them following me, and letting them know I know. When I realized the police were taking aerial photographs of my house from a helicopter, I got a massive picture of my face painted on the roof. There's a 20-foot speech bubble coming out of my mouth and it says, 'What are you fucking looking at?' It cracks me up thinking of what the chopper copper told his sarge back at the nick. 'You'll never guess what Courtney's done now…'

When you're a policeman you're meant to play it by the rule book, but you do get cocky policemen and cocky criminals, so this really struck a chord with me. I've had loads of meetings with policemen in restaurants to wind them up or give them a false tip-off (and I've got all them encounters on tape), but every so often you have to tip your hat when they get one over on you.

When I was about to be nicked a few years ago, the police turned up mob-handed and was just about to pounce on me in my house, when a limo pulled up and whizzed me off to Manchester for a book signing. Imagine that. They were planning to nick me here dead on five, but at ten to, this happened. Suddenly everything's up in the air so they've had a think – and God that must have been painful – and they've all shot up to Manchester as well.

Now, I take my hat off to this one copper because I would have done exactly the same if I was him. There was a queue going out the shop and round the block for this signing, and I'm rattling through them dedicating books to people's husbands, their mates, their dogs and all that. Then this geezer come up to me and went, 'We've got this old fella down the pub who fucking loves you. He's our favourite, he's been going there donkey's years, and everyone in the pub loves him. Can you sign a book for him?' So I've said, 'Go on then, what's his name?' And he's gone, 'It's Bill. Just put, "To my favourite, old Bill, blah blah blah.' So I've done that and he's gone away chuffed. Half an hour later I've finished the visit and I'm being driven down the motorway by my mate Ebo, who now runs a sunbed shop in Welling High Street called Tantalising. I'm actually in the back of the car fucking Jenny, and she's going up and down when she suddenly says, 'We're being surrounded by football hooligans.' We was in the middle lane and there was a car with a load of geezers in on either side of us and one behind. Then all of a sudden this light just came on from over the car like fucking Close Encounters and this helicopter's swooped up and pulled us over. It actually hovered in front of us at 100 mile an hour and made us stop. Proper impressive when you think about it. So we pull over on the hard shoulder and all these red dots are on the car from the marksmen in the chopper, and they're yelling, 'Get out of the car with your hands up.' Jen's pulled her skirt down but I'm stark bollock naked. But as I've bent down inside the car to find my pants they've thought I'm going for a gun so they've gone mental. 'Get out of the fucking vehicle – NOW!' I said, 'I'm not dressed', and I've opened the door. 'The only thing I've got on is a hard.' See them try to work that one out. Anyway they surrounded the car then over steps a guy I recognize from the signing and he's waving his book, open at the dedication page. And I've just laughed. He's got a signed book from me and it says, 'To my favourite old Bill – Dave Courtney'. That's an excellent touch, so hat's off to him. The cunt.

But they do do that, they really do. That's why Pacino pulling his mark over for a cheeky word just rings so true to me because the best policeman is someone who thinks like a criminal and the best criminal is someone who thinks like a policeman. That means you've got a whole lot of people running along the same lines. It doesn't matter what side of the fence they're on, cos they're both playing exactly the same game. It's like David Beckham and Arjen Robben. They both play football and put some wicked crosses in, but they could actually swap shirts and do exactly the same thing for the other side. Fuck me, I've impressed myself with that metaphor.

Everyone's playing the same game now. We all cheat. Us lot lie and cheat to get out of trouble, and make up witnesses and alibis to say we were somewhere when we weren't. The police do the same thing and produce witnesses who say you were there when you weren't. You understand what I mean? The good cop is a very rare one now because it's a lot more productive and a fuck load easier to be a cheating one. If you can't find a witness, a good cop would go to court and say, 'I couldn't find a witness but I can feel someone's out there.' Whereas your average one would get an informant and go, 'Right, you can have ten grand if you come up and say you saw this.' And then it's case closed, the copper's got an empty in-tray and he can finally take his missus on holiday to try and save their marriage.

There's another bit of showmanship in Heat which is just like my little joke with the helicopters. Pacino's team have got De Niro under 24-hour surveillance, trying to second guess what the big job is he's got planned. So after the villains have left this empty warehouse on the edge of town, Al and his boys pile in and have a look at potential targets. There's fuck all out the windows so what could Bobby be looking at? And then he twigs. It's him. On a building over the road, De Niro's laughing to himself with a pair of binoculars as he watches these cops he's smoked out scratching their heads. Real crime's full of all these games.

The big action scene in the movie is the massive bank robbery at the start. They've got the choppers out, the Uzis and Kalishnikovs, and there's a massive stand-off with the police.

> **He's a premier division professional. No baggage, no ties, no drugs problem, so no erratic thinking.**

The thing is, you don't get many bank robbers in England where they go to work in the morning with an AK-47, looking like Brad Pitt, driving a Cobra and having a shoot-out. But in America you do. Them things really happen out there. Remember that film where they showed the first ever armed robbery where they used automatic weapons. They covered themselves in Kevlar and just had the shoot-out with the Old Bill in the street. And because they're so up on the TV thing and everything's captured on TV out there you actually get it all live. Anyone does anything naughty, like the O.J. Simpson thing, we all watch it, don't we? It can have an adverse effect that television thing. Once you know you're going to be beamed to millions of people you could get the 'Omigod, I mustn't be seen doing anything naughty' look. Or the 'Here's the chance to make a name for myself' one.

When they're in the restaurant talking to each other, they both admit it's a bit of a passion with them, and that's true an' all. One was born to be a cop and wouldn't want to do anything else, the other was born to rob and that's his lot too. And now they've come face to face, it would hurt each of them to plug the other one, but they'd still do it. You can't afford to let anything get in the way of business, whichever side you're on. That's why Pacino's screwing up his home life and De Niro's a free man. Like McCauley says, 'Don't let yourself get attached to anything you are not willing to walk out on in 30 seconds flat if you feel the heat around the corner.' And that's top advice.

So why the fuck don't he take it?

The thing that makes De Niro's villain so impressive is he knows what he's doing. He's a premier division professional. No baggage, no ties, no drugs problem so no erratic thinking. I would actually say he was a hero among villains as a good representative of the baddy world. But the problem he's got and the writer's got, is the society we live in. I know to

my personal cost that you cannot, whatever you do, be seen to glamorize crime. So the downside of a lot of films is they spend 87 minutes glamorizing the gangster world and making you side with the criminal, then in the last three minutes they have to make it look like crime don't pay or they lose their funding.

So Scarface has him running out attacking the world and its mother with a machine gun in the end. Goodfellas has the guy turning grass in the final reel. And Heat ends up with De Niro doing something fucking stupid.

Now I've actually made a film myself (see Hell to Pay chapter). I've seen the sort of invisible guidelines that you have to follow in big budget movies. So there's fuck all the writer can do about it:
De Niro's character had to, in the end, do the stupid thing and go back in when he'd got away just to kill the bad guy. In reality, there is no one in the world who'd be that dumb.

The whole film was believable but it fell apart big time there. If someone's that professional, and he's done the job, got away with the lot and got the bird in the car, he wouldn't go back to the fucking hotel for the big showdown that he can't win. That was the only bit in the film that was make believe. They have to make it look like the good guys win in the end and even the best villains make mistakes. But the real world ain't like that, trust me. So do yourself a favour: turn off two minutes before the end and Heat is the best gangster film you'll ever see.

At the end of the day, seeing De Niro and Pacino up there together for the first time is just dreamy, ain't it? These two have done more for villainy in the movies than anyone else. And the weird thing is, it must be getting harder for them to base their characters on real life villains, cos every other criminal in America these days seems to have modelled themselves on them two!

For a young man, Scarface is probably the bollocks. But the older you get, the more you appreciate how real Heat is – apart from the ending.

AND THE MORAL IS...
It's like the song says. 'You've got to know when to hold them, know when to fold them, know when to walk away.' Don't let your heart, or your cock, rule your head and do not fuck it all up at the end and go back.

Vincent Vega by John Travolta

FACTS

JOHN TRAVOLTA PULP FICTION (1994)

DAVE'S FILM FACTS

Written and Directed by Quentin Tarantino. Pulp Fiction rewrote the movie rule book in general and the naughty boys' rule book in particular. John Travolta was dragged back into superstardom with his performance as hitman Vincent Vega and Samuel L. Jackson became a household name thanks to his turn as Bible-thumping badass cool dude Jules Winnfield. The various tales of the rigged boxing match, the date with the mobster's wife, the diner hold-up and the retrieval of the mysterious briefcase were all shown in the wrong order, meaning the film began at the end and ended fuck knows where.

ANYTHING YOU SAY WILL BE TAKEN DOWN…

'And you will know my name is the Lord when I lay my vengeance on you.'

DAVE'S DUSTER-O-METER
INFLUENCE 4
LEADERSHIP 2
SUCCESS 3
NAUGHTINESS 4
AUTHENTICITY 5

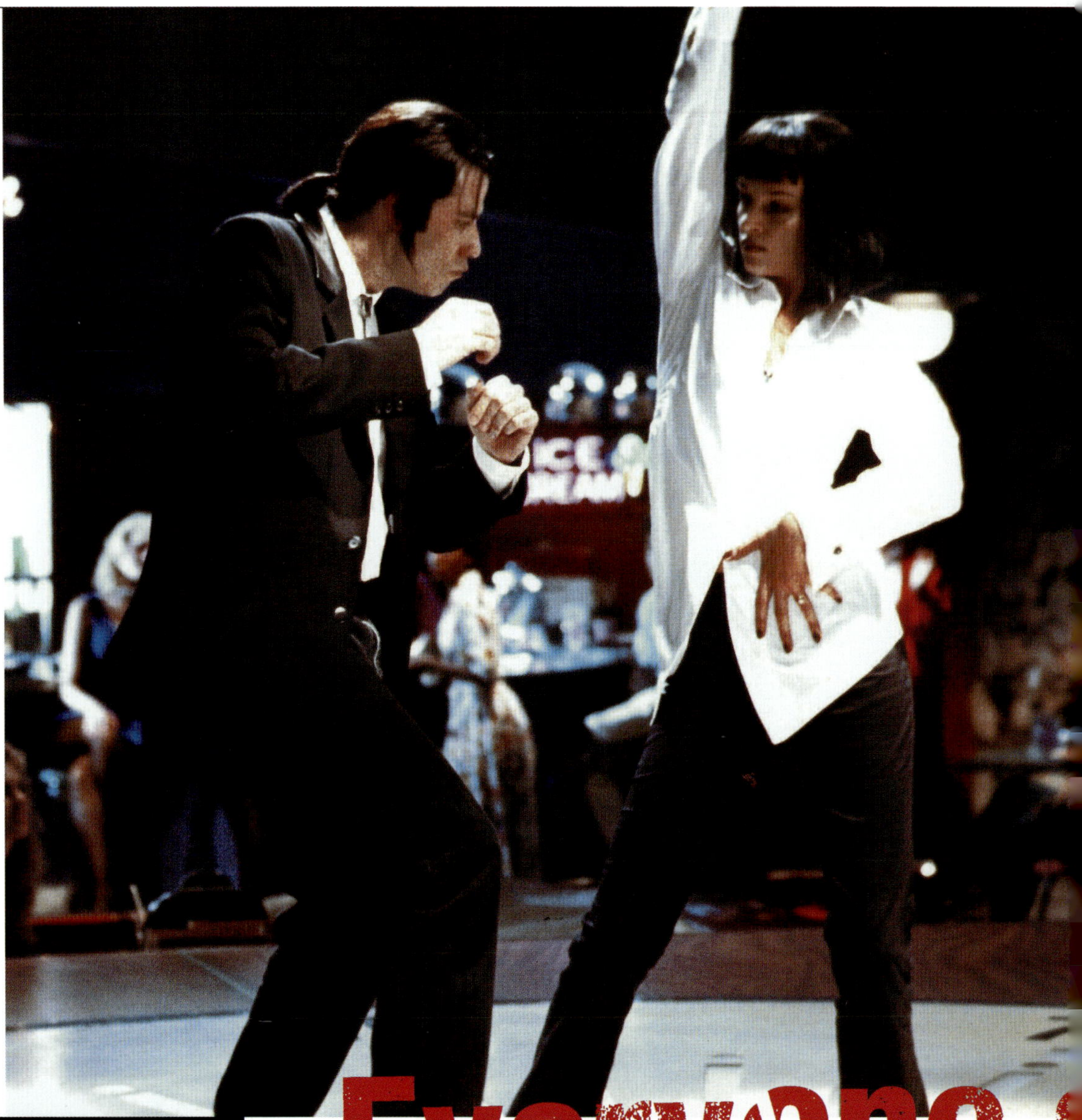

Everyone s
off from wo
no one's s
and gangs
just th

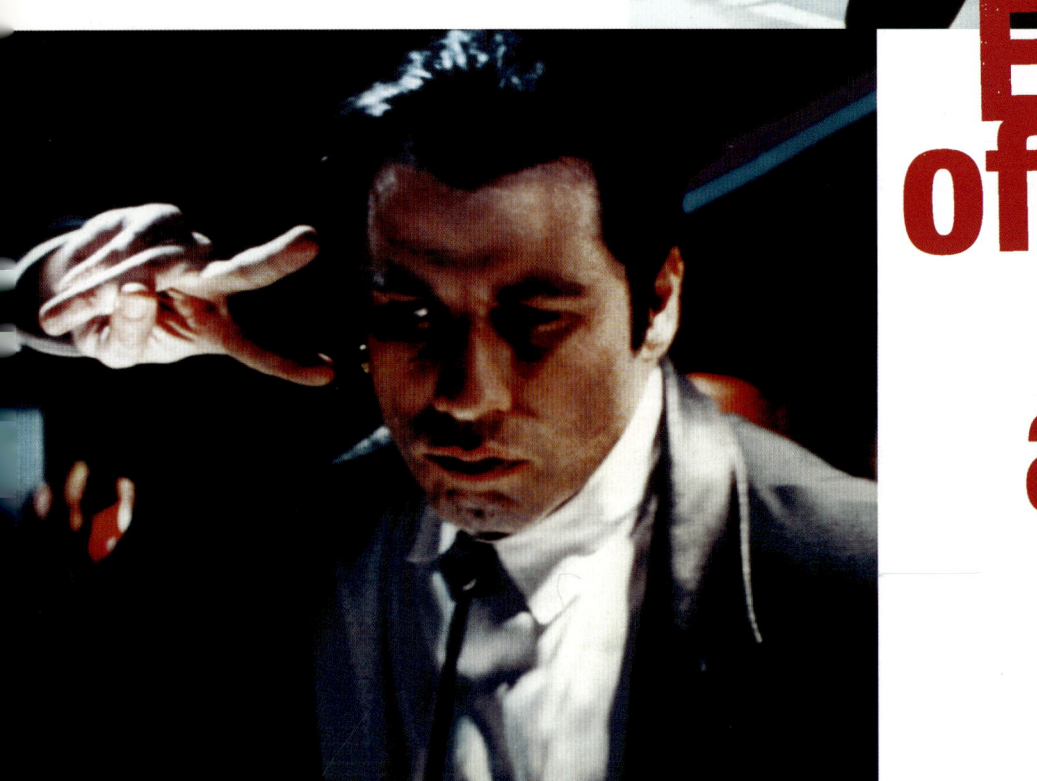

> *I know it looks funny on the screen, but unless you've done that kind of thing as a job, you don't realise how real it actually is.* **DAVE**

Quentin Tarantino's a clever cunt. He can't act his way out of a paper bag, you could land a 747 on his forehead and he can talk for his country but he knows more about using the best bits of old films than anyone else alive. He's a fucking magpie as a filmmaker, but that don't mean he's not the master of putting slices of real life together as well, cos he is. Reservoir Dogs was a good film because it had all the geezers in sharp suits hanging around just shooting the breeze like you do. Should you tip? Yes. Is Madonna a whore? Well, she ain't slept with me. Shit like that.

But Pulp Fiction. That's the bollocks, ain't it? You've got these three little films going on at once and it don't matter if you can't follow what's what, cos they're all really enjoyable in their own way. And, as far as I'm concerned, they're all pretty true to life as well. It might not be your life, but there's someone out there going, 'That's so for real.'

Everyone likes the bit that they can relate to best in a film and the hold-up scene in the restaurant with Honey Bunny and Pumpkin, that seems to get a lot of people excited just cos they'd like to think they could do that. It's reckless, ain't it? You'd have an adrenaline overdose just planning it. But cos it's not in my make-up to stand up in a roadside diner and say, 'OK you motherfuckers, put your money in this bag!' that scene means as much to me as aliens landing on my front lawn. But because I was a debt collector, the work that Vincent and Jules get up to rings my bell big time.

Crime in general is only a job, like everything, and you have a work face, just like the woman selling make-up door to door. She trudges along in the rain and the snow then she rings on your door and it's like a light goes on in her head and – ping! – it's smiles turned up to eleven, 'Avon calling', and you get her work face.

Debt collectors are the same in the opposite way. I have actually driven to places and been talking about McDonald's or football or what car I nearly nicked right up until the geezer opens his door, then on comes the bulldog-chewing-a-wasp look and you're in work mode. Then while they're scrabbling away to get the money, you carry on yapping to your mate about the bird you shagged last night or how far you got on Who Wants to be a Millionaire, and when he comes back you're all snarly and hard bastardy and 'Don't do it again, all right?'

So that bit in Pulp Fiction where they're laughing and joking about the Royale with cheese is so real it gives me a hard on. Everyone around me at the cinema was laughing, but I'm like, 'That's real. That's not a joke.' I know it looks funny on the screen but unless you've done that kind of thing as a job you don't realize how real it actually is. It's just a normal everyday job to them. You might be a milkman delivering a pint of milk or you might be asking the guy for two grand, but whatever you're doing, you're a different person when that door opens. Before it you're just a normal bloke talking to your mate about some piece of skirt. But as soon as it opens you're 'grrrrrr'.

John Travolta and Samuel L. Jackson are pretty realistic cos they play it straight, like crime is a job. And it is. It's not a person or a character or a way of life, it's work. The arguing about being the 'foot fucking master' on the way in, the conversation about hamburgers in Holland, it's all normal stuff that normal geezers yap about on their way to work. Builders do it: 'You remember that time you dropped the brick and it broke in half and we sealed it up and the geezer never noticed?' Or 'What about that time you cracked that window pane so we made the geezer buy a bigger window sill so he couldn't see it.' Everyone switches off from work when no one's looking, and villains are just the same.

Being able to ad-lib when a situation happens will take you further than any other skill.

When I'm debt collecting, I know I've got to knock on somebody's door and be scary enough for him to pay up, but it's no different to being a vet and sticking my hand up a cow's arse all day long to see if it's got piles. That doesn't mean I want to do it at home. For me crime is an ordinary job, but then I can't imagine getting up at six to travel for two hours into London and sit there for another eight asking permission to go to the toilet then another two hours on the way home so my kids are in bed and my missus is too tired for a shag. But people do it. Five days a week for 25 years? Shut up!

And even though it's a bit theatrical, I love that 'And you will know my name is…' bollocks cos I've been in situations where I've launched into one and it means fuck all to the blokes we're scaring, but my mate over there knows exactly what I'm referring to, and we have a laugh about it in the car on the way home. We all have our little things like that to get us through our day. It's no different to a friend of mine doing an interview on telly and making sure my book is on the shelf behind him. Or a footballer might score a goal, lift his shirt up and there's a message on his T-shirt underneath that only his missus will get. There's a few secret messages in this book which only the single person they're intended for will pick up on. We all do it and it just happens to be very effective when you're waving a gun and everyone's laying on the floor. You can come out with whatever shit you want in them situations and I guarantee no fucker will be asking questions.

As long as you're good at the basics of your job, being able to ad-lib when a situation happens will take you further than any other skill. You might be the best typist, the wickedest Corgi gas tester (and that's no job for a dog, especially the Queen's) or something dodgy in the city, but that counts for nothing if you can't produce a bit of blarney on demand, cos planning will only get you so far. You might spend all day thinking of what to say to the

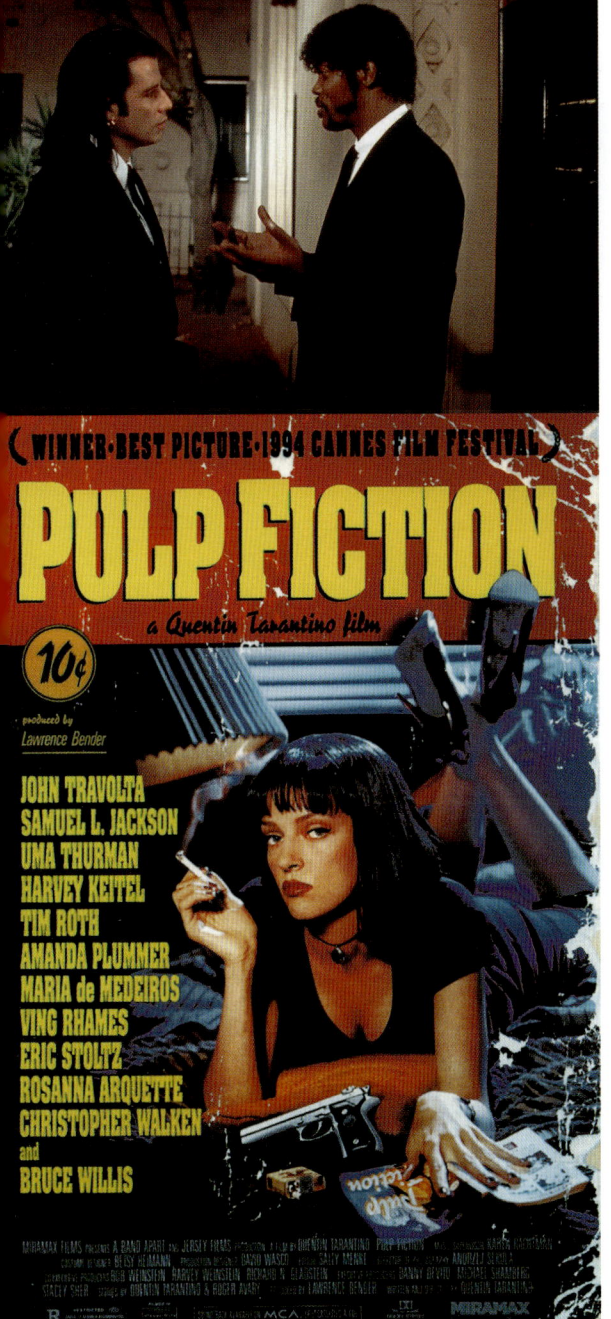

bloke who owes you money, but when you knock on the door he ain't in. Or he might be watching football in the lounge with twenty mates. It's too easy to be wrong-footed if you worry too much about working everything out. The first bank I robbed, I didn't know what I was going to say, and just as well, cos as soon as I stepped in there, all balaclava'd up, everyone hit the floor without me saying a word. There was just this one woman directly in front of me who stayed on her seat, and I said, 'I'd like to make a large withdrawal, please.' I don't know what she thought, but the geezers with me started frothing through their mouth holes. Shut up!

One of the other bits that normally gets a laugh from most people happens to be just as authentic – it's when Travolta's Vincent Vega accidentally shoots the guy in the back of the car. That's not unheard of at all. In normal everyday bricklayers', greengrocers', window washers' lives, you might go, 'Gasp – wow!' But in a criminal's world where they play around with guns all the time, accidents do happen. How many drivers who deliver brand new cars to people have crashed one on the way? I know a bloke who's gone up to a garage at night and tapped on the window with his loaded gun and it's gone off. Blew the guy's head clean off. On the CCTV it looks like he walked up there and – bang – blasted the geezer away for no reason, didn't even ask for money, so they think it's an assassination. And there's people who think they're cowboys and stick a gun down their trousers, not realising the trigger don't have to be right back to fire a bullet. Say goodbye to Mr Testicle… Accidents happen in any line of work. If you're a welder, a gas bottle blows up every now and then and kills someone.

What is a bit special, though, is old Harvey Keitel coming round as the clean-up man Mr Wolf. In England, cos it's so freelancey, there might be two or three major crime firms who have professional tidy-up men – maybe – but in America it's more common. Big organized crime syndicates run their business like the army: one man, one job. If you're a sniper, you don't clean floors. If you're a bridge builder, you don't do assassinations. If you drive a submarine, you're not the guy who primes the bomb and sets the timer. There's a pecking order and every cunt knows his place in it.

The other thing in Pulp Fiction that strikes a chord is the boxing. Like anything in the world, where there is a lot of money involved, there is the likelihood of a scam. And if there is only one person to bribe, I would never bet against it happening. It's very hard to bribe a whole football team – although the German league has had a good go at proving that one wrong recently. But a boxer? Piece of piss.

I know people who throw fights and like Bruce Willis's Butch I've been asked to throw them myself – but it didn't matter cos I was losing anyway. I definitely lost more than I won. Once, I was hit so hard in a fight I was 'meant to win' that I hit the deck and my corner went, 'Stay down till nine.' I thought, Great, what time is it now? I was the only boxer who retired with a cauliflower bum.

Audiences like Butch cos he stands up to the gangsters and runs off with their money. I can relate to him too, cos I've been in his position. Every man would like to have the guts to do what he did. Then it gets a bit messy for him and he shoots Vega, runs over the crime lord he's just robbed then saves him from a gimp. And he gets to say, 'Zed's dead' which is a cool fucking line, ain't it?

Marcellus Wallace stands up very well as a gang leader. He's the epitome of 'the bigger you are, the nastier you are, the more you are in charge' school of thought, but he's also grown into his position and he makes the right decisions. But what the fuck is in his briefcase that is so important I have no idea. As for Jules, he finds religion when all them bullets miss

him and decides to walk the Earth like Cain and I know how he feels. I went to court and was held in the Special Unit in Belmarsh for a year on remand for something I never had anything to do with. They nicked me for a £5 million cocaine seize at Heathrow and called it 'Dave Courtney's drugs ring'. I then realized how many years I could get for doing fuck all, and that made me come out and go, 'Not tonight, Josephine' to all other crimes. I thought, If I get Guilty, by the time I come out of here I'll be too old to be a father. I'll have grey pubic hair!

AND THE MORAL IS…

All that glistens is not gold. The film ends differently for different people and I've no fucking idea what's in the case. We've all got something that would make us go, 'Fuck sensibility, let's have a go at that.' It might be fanny, it might be rent boys, it might be drugs, it might be money. But we've all got something. So by not showing us what it is, Tarantino's been cute and gone, 'There's something that makes killing all these people worthwhile to Marcellus but you'll have to work it out.' The prick.

Big Chris
by Vinnie Jones

FACTS
**BIG CHRIS
LOCK, STOCK AND TWO SMOKING BARRELS (1998)**

DAVE'S FILM FACTS
Written and Directed by Guy Ritchie. Mr Madonna, Guy Ritchie's landmark 'making crime palatable' movie involving as much slapstick as slapping. At least two of the stories (including the title tale) are based on things that have actually happened to Dave Courtney, and it has been said the whole Big Chris character was based on me. Choppy direction, innovative editing and a funky pop soundtrack paved the way for myriad copycat movies.

ANYTHING YOU SAY WILL BE TAKEN DOWN…
Dan: I'll fold.

Phil: Is that the only word you learnt at school?

Dan: No, I also learnt the word 'cunt'.

DAVE'S DUSTER-O-METER
INFLUENCE 3
LEADERSHIP 1
SUCCESS 3
NAUGHTINESS 4
AUTHENTICITY 0

It was a time when criminals were going out 30- or 40-handed, everyone had a Bentley, they had the smart suits, there was the black guys and the white guys together, and there was no trouble with anyone in the clubs.

I've never claimed to be anything other than what I am – I'm just your average author, actor, comedian, hardnut, singer, producer, criminal mastermind, model, love god and leader of men. What I ain't, though, is fucking Businessman of the Year, although I should have won it for this one. See what you think.

It was a few years back and someone rung me up and asked if I wanted to buy two shotguns. At the time I did – I think I must have had a space on my mantelpiece where they'd go nicely, or something. Shut up! Anyway, they were 150 quid each, which I thought was reasonable cos the geezer said they were smart, but he knocked a few quid off cos they didn't look like this year's model. So I've rung back and said I would buy them if he called in on this chap I knew who would cut them down for me. And he said, 'Yes, no problem. You've got yourself a deal.' So a bit later the shooters have turned up, having gone via my mate, and they're now perfectly sawn-off. A nice bit of business, then. Yeah, in Only Fools and Horses, maybe. Cos as soon as I've seen them, I've gone, 'Fuck me, they're antique Purdeys.' They were actually a man and woman set, hand-carved rosewood, made to measure gold triggers and worth about 250 grand as a pair. And we'd just cut them up to make them worth 150 quid.

To add insult to injury, my mate gave me the two end bits they'd chopped off. Let's have a look at what you could have won, and all that. But the way I look at life is any fucker can be the man when things are going well, it's how you deal with the shit that defines you. So what I've done is had them gold-plated, and got two of those big black leather Durexes that you get for a horse, these big fucking sheaths, and put the semi-Purdeys in. Now I've got two golden guns and a fucking rubber Johnny holster. If that ain't the bollocks, what is?

When you go out on the rob, you might take a fucking cannon with you, but that doesn't mean you're gonna use it cos all you want to do is scare the cunt. You just want the nice man to put his loot in the bag, then lay on the floor and let you leave quietly. If you wanted to kill someone you'd be an assassin, so the only reason you get tooled up is to put the frighteners on. I'm actually quite a nice bloke even when I'm on a job – ask anyone I've robbed if you don't believe me. I'm more interested in being a bit showy than nasty, so I thought, What could be more showy than having these two gold-plated bad boys hanging round my hips, and whipping them out in a bank? So that's what I done. It was such a big hit the first time I pulled them out that people got to hear that I had them, and I had to stop using them cos people were learning they weren't all that. But it made me laugh. Maybe not 250,000 quid's worth, but close.

Now if that little story sounds a bit familiar, it's cos you might have seen something similar in a film called Lock, Stock and Two Smoking Barrels. And it just so happens, it's one of many, many stories I told the film's creator Guy Ritchie about my life.

What happened was this: Guy Ritchie was out on the town an' that about ten year ago and on a few occasions we bumped into each other in the West End. At the time the London nightclub scene was pretty much sewn up as mine. I had all the doormen, I was mates with all the owners and the main players and all that, so I should imagine to an outsider it was a very visually obvious power I had. It was a time when criminals were going out 30- or 40-handed, everyone had a Bentley, they had the smart suits, there was black guys and white guys together, and there was no trouble with anyone else in the clubs cos we were keeping it all funny and, I suppose, palatable to the non-criminal fraternity. We weren't going around going, 'Get a load of me,' we was there to have a good time and if we could help other people have a good time, result. People like that, people like us, we're actually an asset to the

clubs. Rather than piling in and being a load of agg, a successful little firm that decided to use your premises as a base could actually beef the place up. The owner suddenly had an entourage, there was a buzz about the gaff and people would actually start to come along just to see it and be part of it. And Guy Ritchie was one of those people so he actually saw Dave Courtney in full flow.

We became friends over a period of time and he couldn't get enough of Dave's World. His parents are something in the local Tory party so he's a nice boy and he ain't exactly used to all the goings on in the underworld that he's made his name from. So his jaw was on permanent drop mode when he was around us cos of the stories we was coming out with, and then one day he said he was gonna make a film about it all.

The next thing I know, he's got me involved in finding him proper hardnuts to make it all authentic, he's roped in Lenny McLean who was working with me at the time, and he's actually got himself a £6 million budget. Crack on.

I was lucky enough to be invited to see an advanced screening of Lock, Stock… and I have to admit I was pleasantly surprised. It's jokey and laughy and not a genuine contender for best gangster movie with its over-the-top action, silly clothes, daft characters and funny scenes, but it was proper wicked entertainment. I love the scene where the guy gets battered with a dildo. But there's no message in it, it's not realistic, you're gonna learn fuck all except how to laugh, but it's good fun and it opened the door for British-made slapstick gangster movies like Snatch, Gangster No. 1, Layer Cake, and programmes like Hustle and all that. It's very watchable, especially as I knew half the characters in it personally and I knew all of them theoretically, cos they was either based on mates of mine or people I've met.

I knew half the characters in it personally and I knew all of them theoretically, cos they were based on mates of mine. **DAVE**

And it weren't just the sawn-off Purdeys story that made it into the movie, either. Years ago there was this BBC documentary made about me called Bermondsey Boy, and in that I tell this story of me and my son Beau going after some geezer who happened to be having a sunbed at the time. What I did to that bloke happens to a character in Lock, Stock… courtesy of a bloke called Big Chris – who seems to have been based on yours truly.

My only problem with it was that they didn't make the guy playing me a bit more flamboyant. But having seen his acting ability, he could not have played me realistically as long as he's got a hole in his arse, could he?

As far as I'm concerned, Vinnie Jones got famous playing me. But I can't see how he could be me in a film and never spoke to me once, never attributed anything to me, never tried to call me, nothing. He must have had Dave Courtney mentioned to him every day, but cos I think his brief warned him to keep his distance cos the producers were worried about glamorizing crime, he never rung me and he never wrote. I even wrote to him but I got nothing back and by then it's embarrassing cos he's going to clubs and asking the doormen, 'Dave Courtney's not here, is he?' and cos they're all mates of mine they tell me. In fact, they tell me they always say, 'Yeah, he is' just so Vinnie fucks off.

When I actually made my own film, Hell to Pay, I wrote to him again, recorded delivery so I know he got it, and I said, 'Look, I know it ain't been easy cos of all the pressures on you to keep your distance, but let's stick two fingers up at them and why don't you appear in my film? You can do what the fuck you want, say what you want, be who you want, and all you have to do is give us five minutes of your time at some point over the next seven weeks.' I thought, seeing as we've both got famous cos of the film, it would be nice for the fans to see us together. I thought it was fair enough. I'm being associated with Vinnie Jones – great. He's being linked to Dave Courtney, and all these doors are opening up for him cos of it. But he never replied, not even to say no, not even through his agent or his manager and from that point on, I must admit I started to hold him in a little bit of disregard. It's very hard for me to say that cos I sound jealous, but I'm not. Good fucking luck to him, I don't hate him, but I don't particularly like the way he does business neither.

The thing is, he might be a convincing hardman to non-hardmen, and maybe out of 100, 95 will go, 'He's good, ain't he?' But the other five who know anything about being naughty will go, 'Fucking queer. He shoots like a girl.' He's an actor who gives it all that with his eyebrows to look hard, ain't he? Anyone who's got to move their eyebrows to look hard can't have it, do you know what I mean? Eyebrows don't fucking scare me!

Anyone who's got to move their eyebrows to look hard can't have it, do you know what I mean?

AND THE MORAL IS...
There is no message in this film. It's a great piece of entertainment and I recommend anyone to go and watch it, but don't think you'll be leaving with any criminal wisdom, unless it's 'be funny'. But if you ain't learnt that from me already, you must be a sawn-off short of a robbery.

Dave Malone
by Dave Courtney

FACTS

DAVE COURTNEY HELL TO PAY (2005)

DAVE'S FILM FACTS

Written and Directed by Dave Courtney. Starring Dave Courtney as gang boss Dave Malone, Hell to Pay explores the complex psychological ties that bind fraternal fealty and – oh, bollocks to that. It's the best fucking gangster film you will ever see. It's real, it's hard, it's hilarious, it's got sex, guns and rock'n'roll and it's available on DVD now!

ANYTHING YOU SAY WILL BE TAKEN DOWN…

'That brief cost an arm and a leg.'
'Whose?'

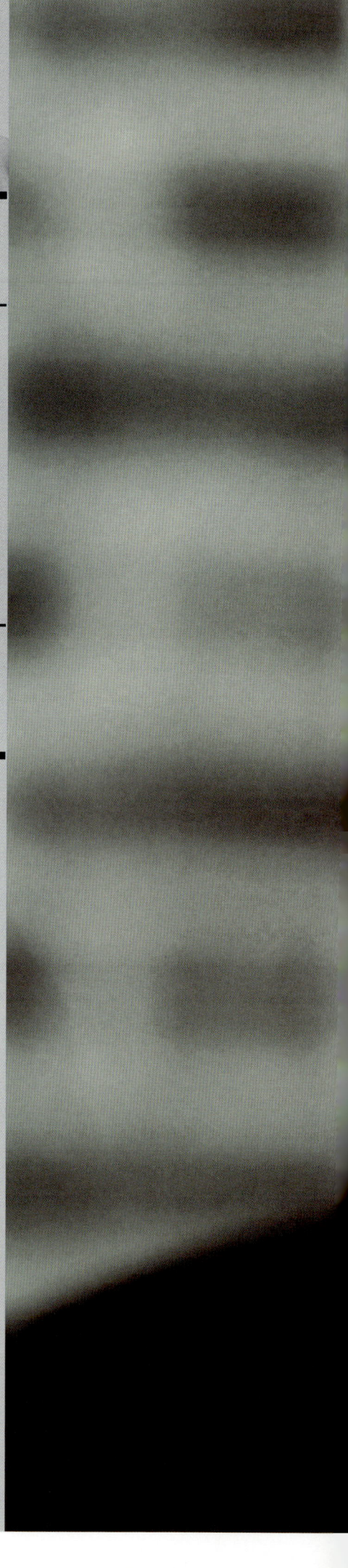

You've had Scarface, Don Corleone, Rico, Capone and Big 'Girl's blouse' Chris. Now meet the real fucking deal: Dave Malone.

That's right, bald-headed, flat-nosed, wise-cracking, head-smacking Dave Malone. He's a handsome cunt, an' all. Lives in this white castle in South London, drives a white Rolls-Royce and knows how to use a knuckleduster. Sound familiar? Well, he should do, cos he happens to be played by me.

I've played in loads of films over the years. Things like Triads, Yardies and Onion Bhajees, which was a winner at Cannes, and Baby Juice Express, which I did with Nick Moran, Joe Bugner, David Seaman, Samantha Janus, Cleo Rocos, Lisa Faulkner and Julian Clary. And that's without mentioning things like Cathula and Lock, Cock and Two Smoking Bimbos, which are for more, shall we say, specialist tastes. Anyway, the thing is, once you've been around film sets a few times, you realize there's a knack to making a movie, like there is to everything else. Whether it's cracking a safe or sweet-talking two birds into your bed at once, it all comes down to practice and a bit of talent. And once you've had that bit of experience, you're fully armed with enough knowledge to make a film yourself. So that's what I done.

Because I've written books, I know that what goes in them is what the authors want to go in them. When I started meeting real gangsters after I'd read their autobiographies, I was like, 'You're a nice bloke and everything, but you ain't that, are you?' When you're the one telling the story, you can fix bits that didn't go right in real life, or give a job a happy ending when it actually went tits up, or make out you was more important than you was. Especially if you're talking about something that happened 40-odd years ago, cos everyone who knows the truth is either dead or can't remember. 'But Frankie Fraser said he pulled this geezer's teeth out with pliers, so he must have done' – yeah, right. Ronnie and Reggie Kray wrote a dozen books

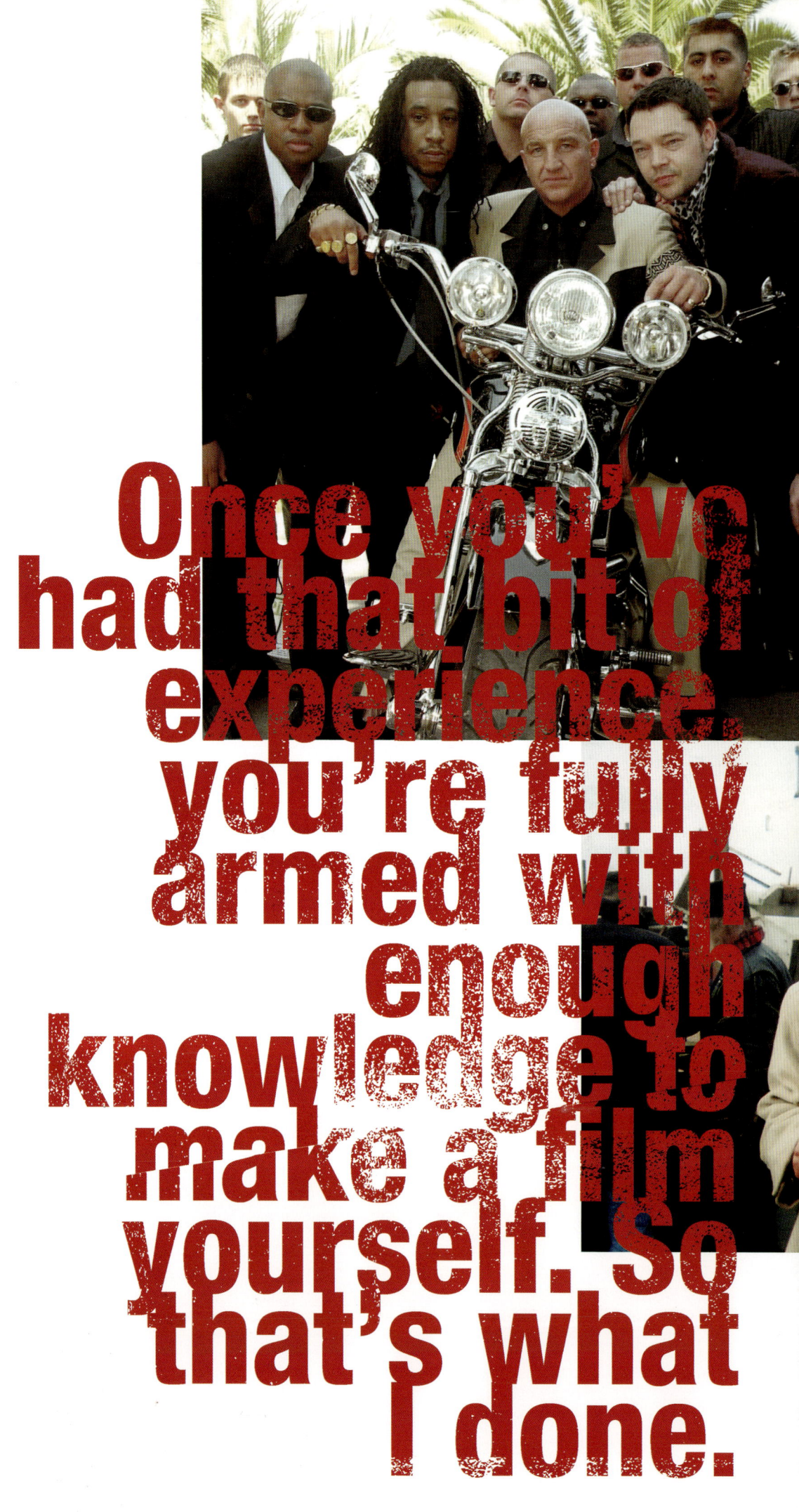

Once you've had that bit of experience, you're fully armed with enough knowledge to make a film yourself. So that's what I done.

between them and in not one did they happen to mention they was raving sausage jockeys. See what I mean?

Well, with films it's a bit like that but a lot more honest. Criminals actually have access to the two best sources of made-up stories in the world. One of them is prison. Because you've got nothing to do all day in there except talk and wank, sometimes at the same time, you get to hear the most fantastic things what people have done or are going to do or nearly did. And even if they ain't true, cos you've got so much time to think about it, in your mind it sort of becomes true so when you come out it's the stories you remember rather than the reality.

The other place that's great for stories is a court. There's nothing like standing in a dock to get the old creative juices going. A geezer might never have touched a book in his life till he's come to put his hand on the Bible and swear to tell the whole truth and nothing but the truth, but once he's opened his mouth he's a better story teller than Jeffrey Archer – although that ain't fucking hard. I've personally come up with enough things in the Old Bailey to keep Jackanory in business for the next twenty years.

So the way you make a film is you get all your mates' best stories and put them all together and make one fucking big story. And then you film it.

I've heard loads of Hollywood superstars talking about how hard it is to make a movie and now I know for myself, cos I done it: it's a piece of piss. The only reason producers tell you it's so difficult is to justify the obscene amounts of money they make and to stop ordinary people like us picking up a camera and shooting our own. But if you've got the right people, let me tell you how hard it is.

Because I've worked on all them other films and been involved in finding locations, make-up,

directing, finding actors, security, editing, producing, doing the soundtrack, lighting, sound and getting hold of the right props (which for Lock, Cock and Two Smoking Bimbos was pretty interesting…), it was really easy to do it for my own film. I had a documentary crew following me around at the time so they could borrow me the cameras and the technical gear. The script was all in my head and most of the actors were my mates. We had Billy Murray from The Bill, Jo Guest, Garry Bushell, Martin Hancock who played Spider in Coronation Street, Mickey Biggs, John Conteh, John 'Nick Cotton' Altman, Robbie Williams' dad, Big Marcus, Dave Legano, Roy Shaw, Joey Pyle, Brendan, Seymour and all the chaps. And we had three months to film it in exotic locations ranging from Plumstead to Portsmouth. What could be simpler than that?

Acting's a piece of piss and don't let Brad Pitt or any other fucker tell you otherwise. If I knocked on your door in the middle of the night and said, 'Do me a favour, tell my missus I was with you last night' – you'd be acting. Without even thinking you'd go, 'Yeah, we was here all evening with a few beers and a Hugh Grant romantic comedy' or whatever, and you would actually be good enough at it to save my marriage. 'Yeah, that's his tissue where he cried at the sad bits and that's where the cunt threw up.' Appearing in court, trying to convince twelve people you didn't do something – when you did – that's acting.

Cos the story and the script was all in my head, the way it worked was every day I'd tell the actors what was going to happen. Then we'd argue a bit, cos all actors are wankers, and then we'd compromise – and do it my way. For fuck's sake, 'What's my motivation for this scene?' Say hello to Mr Duster here. Motivated now?

The thing with acting is, as Hamlet I'd be shit. But I play a fucking good Dave, so that's who I was in the film. I was Dave Malone, my missus played my missus, I wore my own suits, I lived

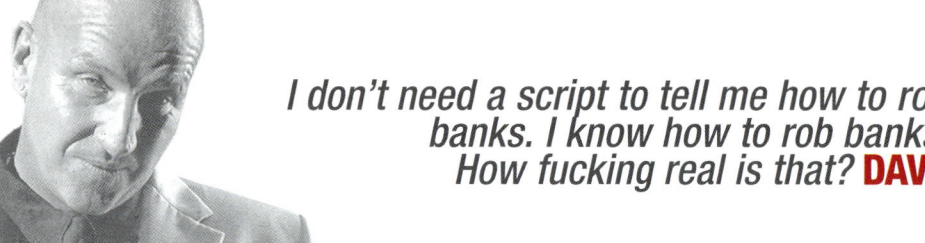

> *I don't need a script to tell me how to rob banks. I know how to rob banks. How fucking real is that?* **DAVE**

in my own house, drove my own car and shot my own guns. How could I not be perfect at that? I don't need to have a script to tell me how to rob banks. I know how to rob banks. How fucking real is that?

And everyone else in the film was like that. You can only get lines wrong if you've got any, but when you're just playing yourself how can you go wrong? So the woman playing a prostitute is a prostitute, the doorman is a doorman, the barman is a barman, the cab driver is a cab driver, the boxers are boxers, the lap dancers are lap dancers and the gangsters are gangsters. And just to prove it, a couple of them never actually finished their scenes due to having to appear in another production down at the local nick. Apparently they'd been doing a bit of out-of-hours practice for their part. That's what I call Method Acting.

Everyone had their normal accents, their normal haircuts and their normal turn of phrase and it totally worked. People say, 'Oh, man, you're such good actors.' I'm like, How do you know, cos none of us are acting.

The plot of Hell to Pay is that age-old one of trust no one, not even your lying toe-rag brother. There's double-crossing, back-stabbing, cheating, stealing, fucking, killing, kung fu mums, big fuck off gun fights and talking to dead people – something for all the family. And it's fucking funny, an' all, which means the authorities will do anything they can to stop people seeing it. My own stab at Oscar glory is where I've got a geezer strung up in my garage and I'm doing some shadow boxing and samurai practice on his head. The camera's just fixed on my face and it's swinging as though you're looking through his eyes on the meat hook and as I'm dishing out the home-made plastic surgery (maybe your nose would look better over there) there's this opera bird warbling in the background. Fucking classy it is. (Which is more than can be said for her record company. 'It ain't going in no Dave Courtney film,' they said, 'it'll be bad for her image.' Ten grand? 'No.' Twenty? 'No.' Twenty-two? 'You got yourself a record, Mr Courtney.' Pricks.)

There's loads of real villain tricks in the film, it's like a masterclass in naughtiness. (So if you're looking for some inspiration for your next job, take a pen and paper and send me a cut from the proceeds.) My favourite is a double-crosser who splashes his trousers so it looks like he's pissed his pants. Obviously his mate lets them stop off to change his kecks, which ain't in the plan, and that's when he gets a new belly button or seven. In his head.

There's double-crossing, back-stabbing, cheating, killing, kung fu mums, big gun fights and talking to dead people – something for all the family.

The other thing I made sure Hell to Pay had was little hidden messages. If you watch any film, you might not pick up on them, but somewhere there'll be nods towards someone or something that ain't necessarily anything to do with the film. Sometimes they're funny. Like getting Sean Connery to play an ex-Secret Service bloke in The Rock just so they can make loads of James Bond jokes at his expense. Or they're respectful: The Godfather's boy 'Sonny' is named after Al Capone's son, and the message they have on the hot air balloon in Scarface is the same one that appeared on a building in the original film. Or sometimes they're little private things like when Tony says 'Look at dem pelicangs fly' – that's actually the phrase Pacino had to practise with his voice coach to learn the accent, but no fucker's gonna know that apart from them two.

So I did things like have Billy Murray from The Bill play the bent copper – cos that's what he played in the series. And as he also plays my big brother, that's another signal cos Big Brother, the authorities and the Old Bill have caused me more problems than anything. But there are a couple of things I've put in that proper crack me up. I've got Ronnie Biggs' son Michael playing a screw in Wandsworth Prison, which is where his dad escaped from. You've got him walking up to a couple of lags and going, 'I've got to go, I've got a train to catch.' And even better than that, there's Dave going to give a slap to a geezer on a sunbed, just like they do in Lock, Stock… The guy going orange says, 'Who the fuck's that?' and I go, 'Well, it's not fucking Vinnie Jones!' How dreamy is that!

I'm not gonna spoil the ending for you, but if you want to see 200 geezers with automatics, sawn-offs, pistols and long coats chasing each other around a submarine yard, you're not gonna be disappointed. Does Dave Malone win? Shut the fuck up.

AND THE MORAL IS...
Trust your instincts. If someone looks like a shifty cunt and acts like a shifty cunt then he is a shifty cunt. If you think someone's having you over, he probably is. Even if it's a copper and it's your own brother.

Villains

VILLAIN

The Krays
Twin Towers

FACTS
THE KRAYS
TWIN TOWERS

DAVE'S DODGY DOSSIER
The Krays are the most famous gangland villains to emerge from Great Britain thanks to their early brand of arrogant violence, their grip on London's East End at the time and the publicity-hungry way they went about their business. Sentenced in 1969 for a recommended 30 years each, Ronnie and Reggie's influence in the criminal fraternity actually increased, with a generation of fans who were not even born when the Krays were free men, buying the twins' books, watching their films and carrying the flame in their name. When Ronnie died in 1995, Dave Courtney memorably organised and ran the funeral in front of crowds of 250,000.

THEIR DODGIEST DAY
The murder of Jack 'The Hat' McVitie. The death of George Cornell had announced the fact that the brothers weren't afraid to kill in public. When Reggie's gun jammed he killed Jack the Hat with the cutlery laying around in the Blind Beggar. There was no shortage of grasses who pointed the finger and the twins got 30 years.

The turning point in my life came when Reggie Kray asked me to organise security for his brother Ronnie's funeral in 1995. Just because the cunt was dead didn't mean the police wouldn't try to fuck him over a bit more, and word was there might have been some less than spontaneous 'anti-Krays' behaviour during the funeral. There was even a whisper that some toe-rags had plans to desecrate the body before it left W. English & Sons in Bethnal Green, so I arranged 24-hour security inside the chapel, with my boys vetting anyone who wanted to come in and pay their respects.

I'll let you into a little secret here: that gig weren't as straightforward as it sounds. Normally when geezers like us are in a room with a dead bloke it's cos we either just topped the prick or we're working out how to lose the body. To actually intentionally hang around a stiff for three days went against every natural instinct we had, so really they was lucky no one panicked. 'Er, sorry, Reg, your brother's at the bottom of the canal.' You know what I mean?

Knowing what I do about police tactics, I would not have been surprised if some uniform had turned up and tried to nick us for murdering old Ron in the first place.

Actually being asked to front the Kray proceedings was considered a bit of an honour for me, but what really gave me the fucking horn was looking out my window on the morning of the funeral and seeing 150 of the biggest hardnuts in the country, all waiting to jump – or thump – on my command. I thought, 'Christ, forget the East End of London – I want to invade Iraq!' How dreamy is that? My own fucking army of flat-nosed, bald-headed geezers, all Crombie'd up and ready for work. You couldn't breathe for testosterone out there. The whole day went off perfect. All the black horses, the carriages, the thousands of people lining the streets. It was like a naughty version of the Lord Mayor's Parade. And yours truly was suddenly a household name.

When you've got a quarter of a million people lining the streets of the East End, for that one day you really could believe everything you'd ever heard about the Krays.

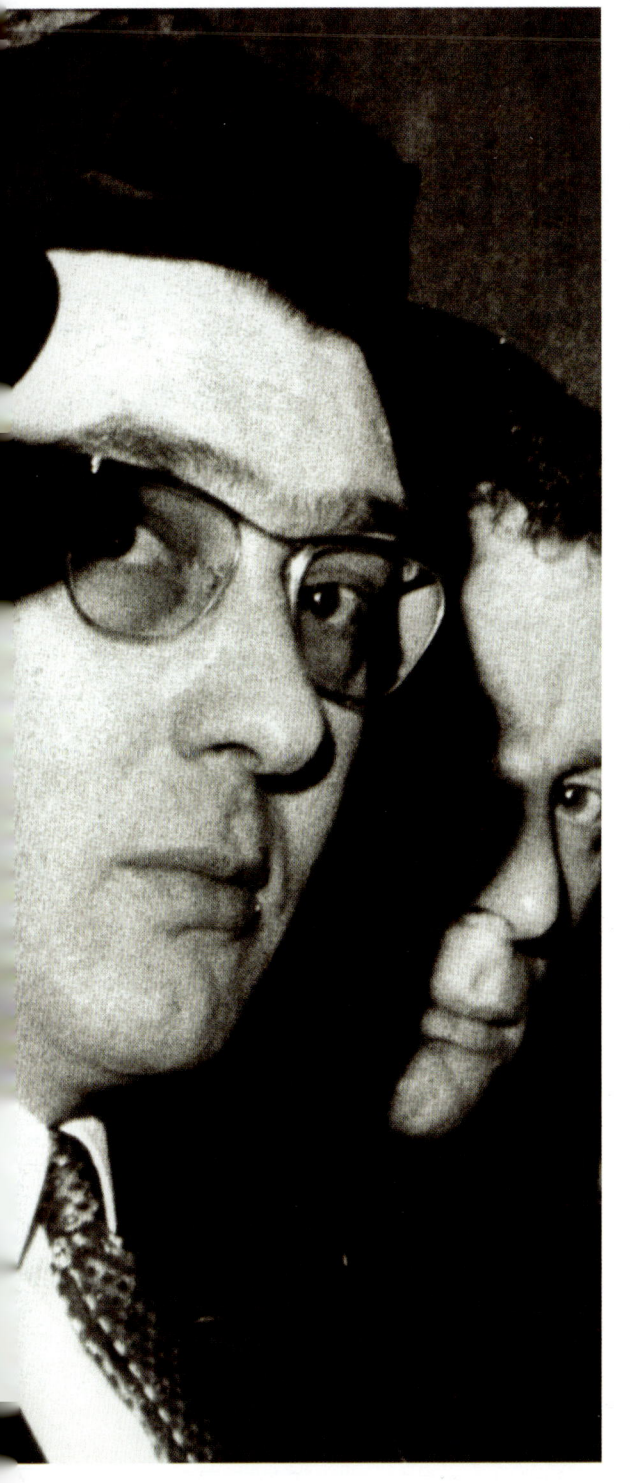

When you've got a quarter of a million people lining the streets of the East End, for that one day you really could believe everything you'd ever heard about the Krays and that era they made their name in. But actually when you look at it, because a lot of those people weren't born when the Krays were running round, the thing they was actually turning up to pay their respects to was the myth of the Krays rather than the real thing. And the real thing, I'm afraid, is nothing like the myth.

Any old bloke who was there during that era will tell you, 'There weren't no drugs when the Krays was around' or 'You could leave your front door open in them days.' Well of course you could, cos the country had just come out of a war and no cunt had anything to nick. The only reason there weren't no drugs around was cos the twins hadn't worked out how to do it, and as for that 'They only hurt their own' bollocks – they only knew their own. They didn't exactly have the widest social circle, did they, cos when you're a naughty boy you tend to associate with other naughty boys. But I bet if Ronnie Kray was doing a bit of late night shopping in Marks & Sparks and a complete innocent stranger beat him to the last pint of semi-skinned, he'd have had something to say about it. So what these old people are saying is the truth. But like, 'Everyone around was English in them days,' these things had fuck all to do with the Krays, and so a whole generation has grown up hearing these glamorised stories of how Ron and Reg were these like modern-day Robin Hoods.

The thing is, the world was different then and you could get away with a lot more, so even if you weren't leading the queue when brains was dished out, it was a lot easier to look good. Ronnie was inside once for giving a bloke a slap, and Reggie broke him out by going to visit dressed as him, then doing a switch. It's straight out of a cartoon, ain't it? Every time they tried to pin something on Ronnie, he'd pretend he was Reggie and had a cast iron alibi. It's like fucking Keystone Cops.

Now, I know some people reading this might be going, 'Woah, there, Dave, where's your respect?' and to them people I respectfully say, 'Fuck off.' Just kidding. The thing is this: everyone who's naughty still really likes them, of course they do. It's like if you're a footballer you probably hero worship David Beckham for what he's done for the sport. If you like playing with birds you're into George Clooney, if you're into cars you like Nigel Mansell. So all villains, like anyone else, are interested in and are pleased about the growth of the Krays' reputation cos that benefits all of us, especially anyone now selling their criminal past. Whether you're pro or anti them don't come into it. We all owe something to the Krays.

But the thing is, it's not really the men themselves you owe something to, it's what the media done to them and for them. I realise this won't go down too well with the masses who have been raised on the legend of the brothers, but the people in the know, the people who actually met and knew them, they'll know what I mean. And it's this: the media created the myth about the Krays. They knew the truth. They knew Ronnie never really had a big firm. They knew he didn't really have anyone working for him when he was in prison. They knew both their homosexual tendencies. They knew there was no fortune. And they knew when they was separated, they was useless.

They didn't exactly have the widest social circle, did they, cos when you're a naughty boy you tend to associate with other naughty boys.

Like anything else, if you're advertising a football team and you've got a shitty back four, you don't actually say how crap they are – you talk about how good the forwards are. So in glamorising the Krays, a lot of things were publicised that actually hid or disguised the truth. There was a bit of a smokescreen on a lot of things to make them look like genius criminal masterminds, but if you look carefully you realise they were actually quite stupid.

Ronnie was mentally ill. He was a certified paranoid schizophrenic fucking maniac – and he was the brains of the outfit. So what chance did they have? Their whole firm was a recipe for disaster cos the things that Ronnie was interested in weren't necessarily the things that was gonna make them a lot of money, or keep them out of prison. Ron was more interested in being seen to be the scariest cunt in town than actually earning any money from crime, and he actually humiliated Reg publicly for not killing anyone before the Jack the Hat thing. When Ron got put away for three years, Reg tried to build little legit businesses, but when Ron got out he fucked them up.

If they'd been a bit smarter, the Krays really could have become what everyone thinks they were. They might not have realised it, but they were seen as a threat by the police because they ran their firm in the same way as the authorities run their set-up, and they had the support of the masses in East London. That means they actually had a mechanic, they had a barman, they had a prostitute, one of everything, something for every occasion. That's exactly like the Freemasons, it's the same structure. You have the policeman, you have the prison officer, you have the fucking judge, you have the barrister, you can influence anything.

But their hunger for publicity and being seen to be the kings of the underworld became an addiction, which I can fully understand myself being in the same situation. Every time they was in the papers, they got a bit more popular and a bit more respected, which was good for business. But that also became their downfall, cos soon they were thinking more about getting on the front pages than running their little empire, and it don't matter how scared of you people are if you're too busy posing for pictures to go and get some money off them.

But what they didn't see is that the authorities were actually giving them enough rope in the press to hang themselves. It weren't just the good things, all their little naughty behaviour was written up as well, a lot of it made to sound nastier than it was. The Krays lapped it up, cos they were only thinking of today and tomorrow, but the authorities were thinking long-term. They knew they wanted to nick them for certain things and invested their time in using the press to publicise how bad the Krays were then sat back and waited. By the time the police finally got the Krays in court, because they'd spent so much time running them down in the general media, no one said a word when these two East End poofs got thirty years – minimum – for something anyone else would've got fifteen for. It was a proper carve up: they hadn't shot the Queen Mum, they'd actually done the public a favour by getting rid of a couple of nasty bits of work. Thirty years? For that?

Another part of the myth was that they were successful. Guess again. There was no Kray millions. When Reg and Ron went in they was living with their mum in a council house. If I didn't send Reg stamps, he wouldn't have been able to afford to write to anyone. I sent trainers, pens, all sorts to keep them happy, and make their life a bit more tolerable in there, so when Ron died I inherited an original painting he'd done in prison of the crucifixion. I'm not gonna tell you how much that little treasure is insured for but put it this way – how shit is that that Ron's etchings are worth more than he ever earned through being naughty.

If I didn't send Reg stamps, he wouldn't have been able to afford to write to anyone. **DAVE**

It weren't just the good things, all their little naughty behaviour was written up as well, a lot of it made to sound nastier than it was. The Krays lapped it up, cos they were only thinking of today and tomorrow.

Even when I was running round for them I was doing an awful lot better at the time than they'd ever done. I had a little firm with 500 doormen on my books, and I was doing all right. They never had that, even when they was out. They were the worst leader material I've ever heard of. The worst natural leader material. They would break someone out of prison, go to all that trouble, then cos they couldn't afford to feed him and didn't know what else to do with him, they killed him. No fucking clue.

As someone who has people listen to what he says and come to me for advice, the worst thing the Krays ever did, in my opinion, was get their boys sent down with them. How fucking all for one is that?

Until he recently died, I was lucky to have Ralph Haeems as my solicitor for 25 years. He also happened to be the brief for the Krays – although maybe that's not the best advert in the world cos they got thirty years for something that was worth fifteen.

Anyway, the case against them was so strong, Ralph said they would definitely be found Guilty. So the police came to them with this offer and said, 'If you plead Guilty, we'll let your firm off. If you don't, we'll do the lot of you and you'll all go down.' The thing is, prison was a lot nastier then, a lot more dangerous. So the twins have had a little conflab in front of their solicitor and gone, 'The truth is, we are both midgets, homosexual midgets at that, and a lot of people are just gonna want to have a look at our reputations for being tough and take a pop at us. Since we're going to prison anyway, do we go on our own or do we bring the firm with us?'

That's not fucking leader material!

Believe it or not, it gets worse. The rest of the firm, good men like Tony and Chris Lambrianou, Charlie Kray, Cornelious 'Connie' Whitehead, Ronnie Bender, John 'Ian' Barrie and even Freddie Foreman all got 15 years – but 24 months in, Reggie wrote a book and admitted it. Every fucking thing. So they're now going, 'We got fifteen so you can write a book? Why didn't you admit it 24 months ago, you prick?'

But the person I feel most sorry for was Charlie Kray. He wasn't a villain, he wasn't a gangster. He got two sets of ten years down to them. Imagine it, he's ticking along nicely as a normal twelve-year-old kid and his mum gives birth to fucking Ronnie and Reggie Kray. What the hell's that about? Thank you, God! So he can't even go out and get a proper job cos his brothers are gangsters but he's not a gangster himself, so he's now skint, holes in his shoes, Casio watch and all that.

His downfall was he was a proper 'champagne Charlie' and cos he hated to disappoint he ended up promising things he shouldn't have in exchange for a drink. So if you went to him, 'Charlie, can you get us a gun?' he'd never go, 'Sorry, I'm not a gangster.' He'd go, 'Yeah, yeah, give us a drink and I'll have a chat with the boys, give us a bell Monday.'

'Charlie, I need someone to have a word with my neighbour' – 'Stick a large brandy in that and consider it done.'
Murderer, lost cat, Scud missile – it was always, 'Yeah, I'll have a chat with the boys – mine's a large one, by the way.'
Course, one day it's 'Charlie, can you get me a ki of coke?'
'Course I can. Your round, is it?'
'Can you get me one a week?'
'No problem. I'll have a chat with the boys. Stick a double in there, would you?'
'When can I pick the first lot up?'

So then he's in a fix and before he knows it he's up for smuggling drugs worth £56 million. And cos his name's Kray Charlie's immediately slung in the Special Unit while he's waiting for his trial. And that's a proper pisser cos that part of Belmarsh Prison is purely designed to make the jury think something without the police actually telling them.

By the time I got to see the twins they were 60 years old and they'd both mellowed in their opinions. But we still had our arguments and I don't really do the 'know your place' thing so I gave as good as I got. I wasn't 'yes, sir, no, sir' when they was alive and pissing on their graves just to sound hard once they're gone. I always made sure I said things to their faces, so that's why I'm entitled to say things that might sound a bit against the grain now. So yes, all criminals like myself owe them a huge debt, but a lot of their mythology was created by themselves. I mean, Ronnie wrote five books and in all of them somehow forgot to mention he was an iron.

AND THE LINK IS…
Everyone knew Ronnie was gay, but it was less commonly known that Reggie was as well. He used to get all these little gay boys in prison, get them out of their heads, buy them trainers and all that, just to make them a bit more friendly. So I was actually paying for his blow jobs! Stop it! Cos it was my job to actually go around all the press and make sure they never ran these sort of stories, they all thought I was a heavy for the Krays – when really and truly I'm involved in a gay porn shagging ring.

VILLAIN | 102

The Richardsons
Brothers with Arms

FACTS

THE RICHARDSONS BROTHERS WITH ARMS

DAVE'S DODGY DOSSIER
In 2004 the Richardsons' life was turned into a film called Charlie with Charlie played by Luke Goss. The Kemps as the Krays, Bros as the Richardsons – what is it with pop star twins who think they're gangsters? What next? The Cheeky Girls starring as the Gambinos?

THEIR DODGIEST DAY
What do you think? The whole Kray firm going away. What a fantastic thing for Manchester United if all the Chelsea players got shot. Know what I mean? Fucking hell, what an easy division it would be to play in then.

DAVE'S DUSTER-O-METER
INFLUENCE 3
LEADERSHIP 4
SUCCESS 5
NAUGHTINESS 5
MYTHOLOGY 3

> The Richardsons were shipping money out of Africa by the boat-load while the Krays were still living at Mum's

Now this mob were the real McCoy. They were a proper firm. Intelligent, naughty and hard – the perfect mix – at a time when most outfits struggled to get two out of three. Fuck, most outfits couldn't count two out of three.

You know they were good cos they made an awful lot of money – and that's not as common as you think in the crime world, whatever the Daily Mail might try and scare you into believing. I'm currently in talks with a famous film director to play a bank robber in one of his new films and he's talking about paying me for the privilege. That's more than I made when I robbed banks for fucking real!

Not only did the Richardsons make money, they actually kept hold of it cos they were always worried about the long-term, not just impressing some birds for the weekend. So they had loads of things going for them, loads of proper little earners, not just the showy stuff like nightclubs and casinos. They had a breaker's yard that actually made legit money for the taxman to look at, but their real business was in the diamond mines in South Africa. Imagine that. Most firms at the time couldn't find South London, yet this mob was digging up the other side of the world. But it weren't just the criminal fraternity who didn't have a fucking clue about all that – Johannesburg weren't exactly on the average bobby's beat neither, so they got really left alone by the Old Bill.

The Krays were silly in comparison to the Richardsons. Ronnie and Reggie didn't really own the nightclubs they fronted, they were more interested in getting in the papers and leaving the money-making to other people. The police gave them an awful lot more credit than they deserved, and enhanced the myth of what they weren't. And once the police give you the credit, the public believe it as well. The Richardsons were very, very aware of all this and hid behind the Krays' publicity. You know like a naughty kid in school gets all the teacher's attention so the rest of the class can do what the hell they want? It was like that. The Krays were running around being noisy, brash fucking cartoon villains, and the Richardsons actually used it as a smokescreen to get on with their own business.

The Richardsons were shipping money out of Africa by the boat-load while the Krays were still living at Mum's. It don't take a lot of working out who was best. But that's not how the average person remembers it, is it? Ask anyone about the old time gangsters and it's Krays this, Krays that. The Richardsons are definitely second when it comes to the mythology thing.

But the thing is, mythology is full of what's been written about at the time. The Richardsons were clever and the last thing they wanted was to be famous. If you're known, crime is virtually impossible. Look at me – I can't go into a bank to open an account these days without the bird behind the desk sticking her hands in the air as soon as she cops me. 'But I want to put money in!' So the gangster legends of today actually just reflect the noisiest cunts of the past and the fact they was being so openly naughty people were interested so they wrote about them. If in Biblical days the guy banging the Lord's lessons into the tablets was an Arsenal

I know the Richardsons very well and anyone who was lucky enough to be their friend felt it an honour, cos they was good people. **DAVE**

The Richardsons were clever and the last thing they wanted was to be famous.

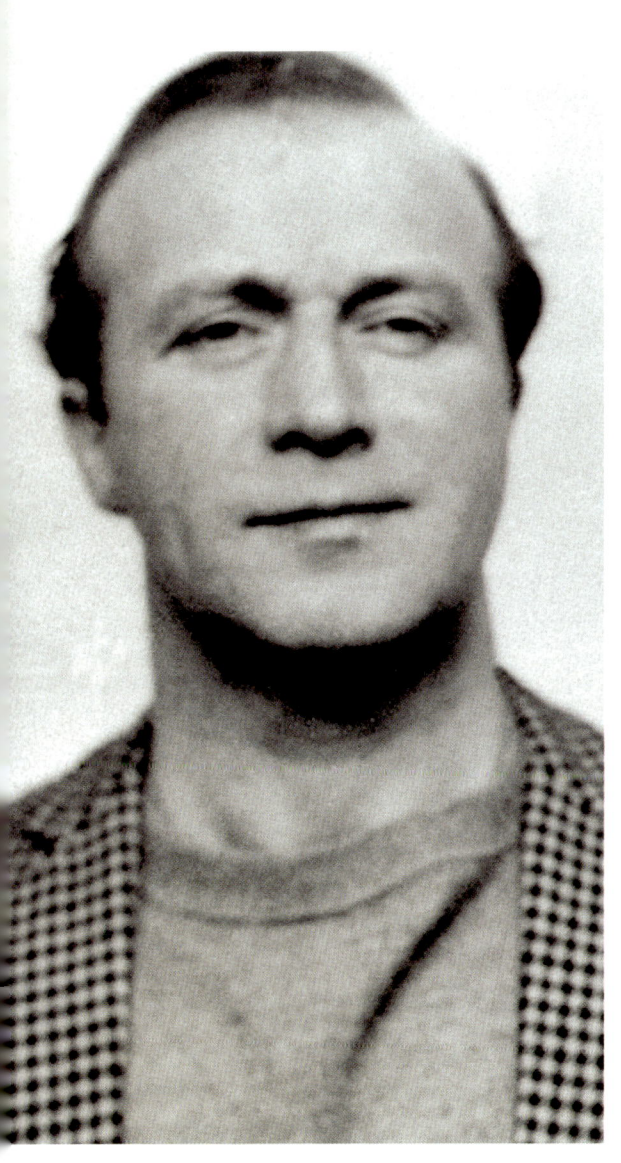

fan, everything you read about now would be about Arsenal. They might not be the best, but he's the geezer with the pen – or the chisel – so that's what's passed down. You get what I mean?

The only mythology the Richardsons was interested in was if it helped their business. They didn't care about some housewife in Hull reading about how scary they was over her cornflakes. So what if they're the main headline on the World Service – that's a fucking bad thing, right? But if they could give a leg up to their reputation among the criminal fraternity, that's another matter. So when Frankie Fraser got the nickname 'The Dentist' (do I really need to explain how?), it suited them cos suddenly their firm was known to have a torturer on their books. That was proper scary.

The thing is, he's admitted and they've admitted that no geezer ever got his teeth pulled out with pliers. But the Richardsons had the benefit of being seen to be a lot more don't-mess-with-us than they was, and Frankie, who was only a little fella, could walk around and not get beat up cos he was known as one of the Richardsons' main men. It was an amicable set-up.

I know the Richardsons very well and anyone who was lucky enough to be their friend felt it an honour, cos they was good people. I probably know Charlie a bit better, and he is a lovely fella. If you met Charlie now you wouldn't believe there was an ounce of naughtiness in him. He is an honourable man and that's how they ran their firm. Put it this way, not a lot of people got a hiding for fuck all from Eddie and Charlie, not like you could from the Krays. The Krays shot their own blokes, for fuck's sake. There was nothing nice about them at all. They took all the glory for everything all their geezers did. When their bloke Mitchell broke out of prison, all they did was pull up in the car park and pick him up, then killed him cos they didn't know what else to do. Horrible things like that. The Richardsons weren't like that.

Even though they weren't really playing in the same league success-wise, the rivalry between the gangs on each side of the Thames was real enough. That river really, really meant a divide between the South and the East of London. In fact, it only really went away when raving came into this country when hordes of people from all over, all went to the same place. The blacks weren't stuck in Brixton and the whites left their palaces in Hampstead and everyone came and partied at the Ministry. That actually got everyone meeting each other. But before that, that North v South divide was a good enough reason to be shot for.

I never said I was the biggest gangster in the world, but I knew them all. Because I was very close to the Krays and the Richardsons, I was actually very instrumental in bringing Charlie Richardson, Frankie Fraser and Charlie Kray down to meet Reggie Kray in a very memorable meeting in Maidstone Prison. The last time this lot had seen each other 30 years ago, they'd been shooting at each other. But here they was, all holding hands and looking at each other and reminiscing like normal old geezers. It was very emotional and it was really eye-opening cos they was going, 'If only we'd known then what we know now about how the police manipulated things with the papers to get us all fighting each other.'

Even though they weren't really playing in the same league success-wise, the rivalry between the gangs on each side of the Thames was real enough.

AND THE LINK IS…
I was proud to arrange a meeting between the Richardsons, the Krays and Frankie Fraser, especially when I saw how much it fucked up the authorities when they realized it was happening. 'What the hell are they up to?' But to be honest, despite the police's nightmares, the meeting didn't actually achieve nothing. I just wanted them to see each other again before they died.

Joey Pyle
Boxing Clever

FACTS
JOEY PYLE
BOXING CLEVER

DAVE'S DODGY DOSSIER

Mr Unlicensed Boxing himself, Joey Pyle's colourful career stretches back to the 60s and his days running gambling clubs in Soho and hanging out with the number one Family in New York. You name it and Joe was involved in it. Then, as now, Joe was the guy people wanted to be seen with: from Diana Dors, Oliver Reed, Joe Louis and Reggie Kray back then, to the likes of E17 and Mark Morrison recently. He is on the straight and narrow these days, but Joe was lured out of retirement a while back to take part in a TV show called Heist where villains were hired to nick stuff to order. Him and a few mates turned the art world upside down by swanning off with a million-dollar painting. Talk about taking candy from fucking babies.

HIS DODGIEST DAY

What do you think? Three men enter a room, two walk out and one leaves in a box. Johnny Nash says it weren't him and he didn't see who did do it. Joe Pyle says the same. Gangsters 1 – The Police 0.

DAVE'S DUSTER-O-METER
INFLUENCE 3
LEADERSHIP 4
SUCCESS 5
NAUGHTINESS 4
MYTHOLOGY 3

I know he's on my 'villain' list, but Joey Pyle is one of my closest friends and someone who I would always defend and admire. He has been a proper figure in the London crime scene since the 1960s, although I wouldn't say he was a major criminal, more a premier division referee. Having said that, there was one little episode that cracks me up today.

The Nash family were definitely, definitely, definitely a force to be reckoned with in the '60s, without any shadow of a doubt. All three of them went to prison for murder although now they're all successful property developers. But one day Johnny Nash and Joey Pyle was in a room together and one other person went in that room. There was a gunshot and Johnny Nash and Joey Pyle walked out. In court, Johnny Nash says, 'I didn't do it, and I didn't see who did.' And Joey Pyle says, 'I didn't do it, and I didn't see who did.' So what do the police do now? They can't put both men in prison, cos only one of them pulled the trigger, can they? So they had to let them both go, which I think is absolutely fucking wicked. That's playing the law, innit?

Unfortunately, the police don't like being made pricks of, even though it's just so tempting and so fucking easy! Just look at Kenny Noye. Remember when he was all over the press for having a phone in prison? Everyone's got a phone in prison. Everyone. But as soon as they caught him with one it gave them an excuse to say, 'It's an escape attempt and we can lock him up in solitary confinement again.' It was pure propaganda. It's all because he killed a policeman.

> **He has been a proper figure in the London crime scene since the 1960s, although I wouldn't say he was a major criminal, more a premier division referee.**

The difference between Joe and a lot of the old villains is there was money actually made there. I'd say 90 per cent of criminals end their careers with no money. **DAVE**

And that's what I think happened to Joe. Someone who worked for him walked in and asked to buy a ki of heroin and he went, 'I don't do that.' Then a bit later someone else walked in and offered to sell him some at a stupid price and he went, 'Hang about, I've got a buyer for that.' So he done the deal and it turned out to be a set-up by the police and they nicked him for it and he got twelve years. How naughty is that? And all because of that time when he walked out of a murder scene and went, 'I didn't shoot him and I didn't see who did…' The police have long memories.

But Joe was a main player. He had his own little firm and they covered London in general, plus Soho. Everyone was trying to nick a bit of Soho at the time, so they all had their own manor, and Soho. The Richardsons were the only ones who went, 'Have Soho, we want the fucking South African diamond mines, you pricks.'

As you can tell from the little 'it wasn't me story', Joe was really close to the Nashes, they were very tight. They were on a par with each other and did their own things, but together they was like one firm. You know how you get different motorbike groups today, so some bikers go with the Angels, some go with the Outlaws? Well the Pyles and the Nashes all went together. He was actually running a casino in London with Johnny Nash when the Krays went to him and said, 'Can we front this casino? We don't want money out of it. If the shit hits the fan, we take the blame, but can we say it's ours?' They just wanted the publicity. So Joe went, 'Yeah, fucking right you can, you silly cunt.' They was more interested in getting photographed in the papers with Liza Minnelli.

The difference between Joe and a lot of the old villains is there was money actually made there. I'd say 90 per cent of criminals end their careers with no money. They must have regrets but whether or not they admit it is another

In court, Johnny Nash says, 'I didn't do it, and I didn't see who did.' And Joey Pyle says, 'I didn't do it, and I didn't see who did.' So what do the police do now?

> **He probably had the best fighters in the country on his books at the time, but cos they were forced to keep it all underground, there was no fucking way on this Earth that one of them would ever be allowed to represent England.**

thing. They've gone through all these things, done their thirty years and had all the shit, and most of them have no bank balance to show for it, but whether they admit that I don't know. When you look at it, crime didn't exactly pay for the Lambrianous, Frankie Fraser, Ronnie Biggs, Bruce Reynolds, the Krays, Roy Shaw, did it? Joe's probably the only active member of the premier division crime world who is constantly in contact with the 'Family' over in America. He had cause to be on the run from the Old Bill a few years ago, so he took his boy, Joey Pyle Jnr, and they hit the States. The naughty world is a lot smaller than you think, and when a quality operator arrives in your town, he might be fucking coughing his guts up cos he's running away from the cops that fast, but you recognize a talent. So it didn't take long for Joe to get in with the top boys over there and that 'working' relationship still continues today.

Apart from the heroin sting, the authorities proper stuck the boot into Joe's legit business, which was as a boxing promoter. Joey Snr was king of the unlicensed end of things, and he actually promoted Roy Shaw and Lenny McLean into the stardom they achieved and was responsible for the reputations they still have today. He probably had the best fighters in the country on his books at the time, but cos they were forced to keep it all underground, there was no fucking way on this Earth that one of them would ever be allowed to represent England. The last thing the police wanted was any legitimate success falling Joey's way – he could have become a national hero, a big name like Mickey Duff or Frank Warren, if one of his boys had been allowed on the same card as the famous heavyweight fighters doing the business for all the belts. So his grittier side of the business never got the recognition it deserved, and all cos of that time he walked out of the room and said, 'I didn't shoot him and I didn't see who did…' You can tell how connected Joe still is by the turnout at his lad's wedding a few years ago. I've known Joey Jnr since he was a boy and we've done lots of boxing promotions together. He's not a criminal or nothing, but talk about an A-list turnout. It was The Godfather meets The Long Good Friday – cos, apart from Lenny who was in hospital, every face from the UK end of the naughty world was there. And knocking back the Bolly next to them was all these slick-looking, tanned, sharp-suited Italian geezers from New York. You get what I'm saying? I'm not really one for the hero thing, but I used to look at these blokes when I was young and want to be like them, not realising they was not actually gangsters – they was retired gangsters. They turned up to the boxing matches with their designer suits, Cuban cigars and a dolly bird on each arm and I thought, I want some of that. But I didn't realize you can only live like that when you're not on the Most Wanted list. When you're doing it for real, the last thing you do is show off and draw attention to yourself (and that's why I weren't that good at it) if you can't prove your earnings. You don't get a silver Aston Martin, you get a beaten up Sierra. You keep your Rolex indoors and go out in your crappiest Casio. You get what I mean? It's only when you've got nothing to hide you can jazz it up a bit. I get the same thing today. People look at me and how I live with the castle and the Rolls-Royce an' that, and they go, 'I wanna be a gangster.' But I'm not actually a gangster – I'm cleaner than I have been all my life.

Joe Jnr still does the boxing promotion today and his dad still puts on these unlicensed bouts. You can buy them all on DVD from his website. But Joe Snr's also involved in the music business now, with Death Row records, with Sugar Night and a load of other things. And closest to my heart, he's got his own security company, a proper load of bald-headed, flat-nosed geezers working for him on the door all round the country. And the best thing of all is it's all legitimate so there's fuck all the police can do about it.

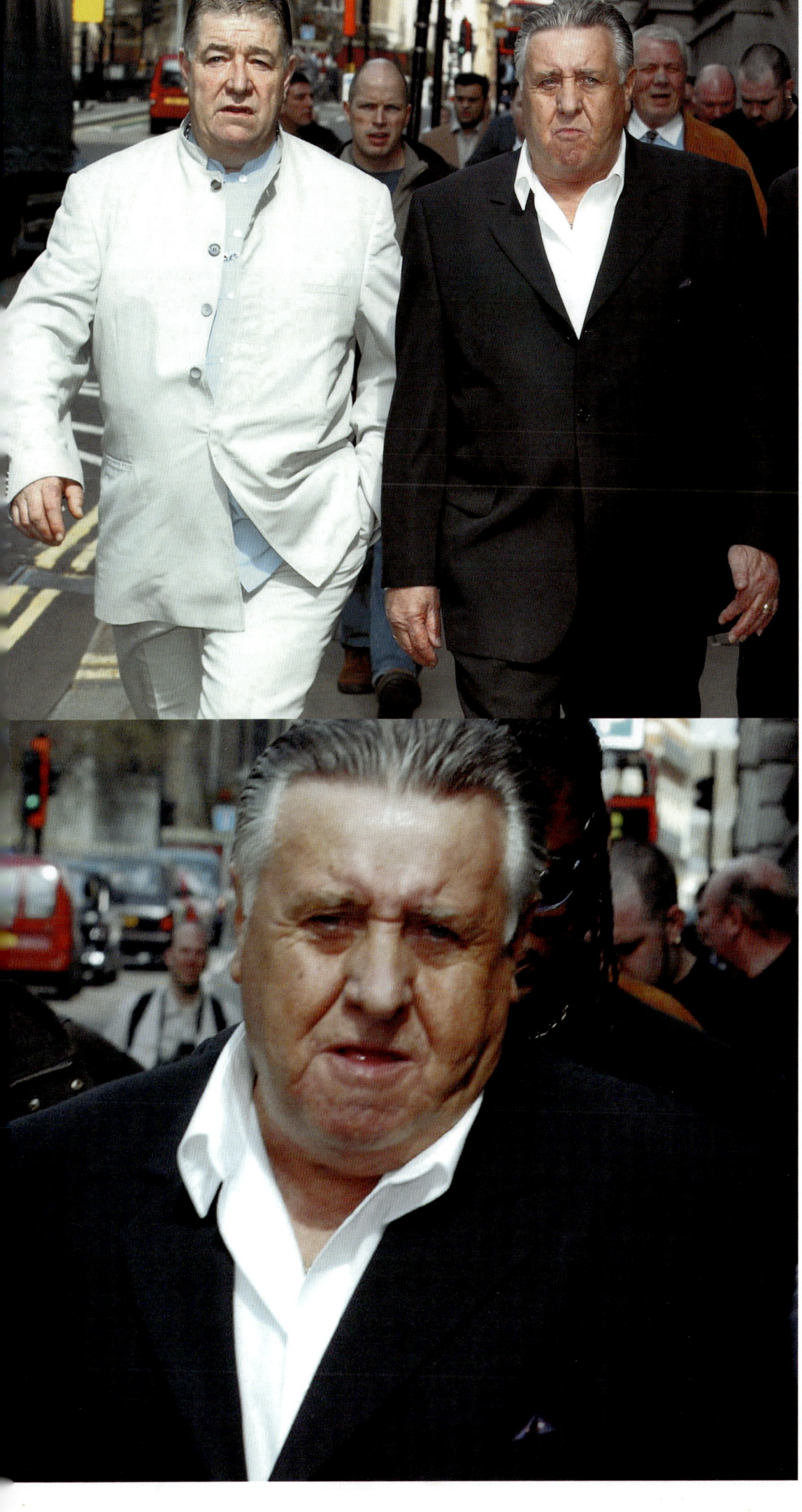

AND THE LINK IS...

Joe's a bit of a public figure these days and he has his own excellent book out. He was actually kind enough to appear in my film Hell to Pay as himself. I had Tony Lambrianou and Roy Shaw and loads of others in there as well, just so I could say there were 70 people in the film who'd done their own books. That's got to be a world record, ain't it?

VILLAIN

John Gotti
The Teflon Don

FACTS

JOHN GOTTI
THE TEFLON DON

DAVE'S DODGY DOSSIER

They don't come more famous than John Gotti. He worked his way up through the Gambino Family by taking care of irritations that the then gang boss had – and making sure no one found the bodies. By the time he became head of the Family, he had every outward appearance of a businessman in charge of any other multinational company. He became a worldwide name when three high profile court cases against him collapsed in mysterious circumstances, earning him the nickname 'The Teflon Don'.

HIS DODGIEST DAY

Three court appearances, three Not Guilties. Only a man who's been in his shoes can understand how good that feels (but since no fucker can afford his shoes, we'll have to guess). The press covered every day of the trials and the police looked like idiots at the end of them. Oh dear, how my heart goes out to them. Stop it!

When it comes to British villains, Americans know two names: the Krays and Dave Courtney – and since the Krays don't do that many chat shows, I'm the one carrying the flag over there for British crime. Over here we've got the same thing. Everyone knows the name of Al Capone and this geezer: the Teflon Don – John Gotti himself.

I mention this bloke a lot, not only cos he's the most famous American gangster of his generation, but cos we actually have a lot in common. I'm not talking about the fact that he was the head of the Gambino Family – fuck me, no one in America could compete with that, let alone a boy from Peckham. I'm talking about his nickname – he didn't get it cos he was good at washing-up.

When you've had fourteen court cases with no convictions, you start to get a bit cocky. I know what you're thinking, 'Dave – how could you get any more fucking cocky?' But listen, I don't care if you like The Beatles, Beethoven or The Bay City Rollers, there is no more pleasing sound to the human ear than the foreman of a jury saying, 'Not Guilty.' If you're prone to public displays of premature ejaculation, I guarantee that's when one's gonna pop out. I must have lost a pint in courtrooms over the years. (A pint? That's a whole armful. Yeah, near enough…)

Anyway, you don't get called the Teflon Don for nothing. Gotti was up for three trials between 1986 and 1990. The New York Police Department, the US Attorney's office in Brooklyn and the state's Organized Crime Task Force all took a shot at the biggest gangster in the US – and they all come off second. You don't know how much that must have fucked the authorities off, cos they'd actually pulled a few strokes of their own to fix the outcome. Do I know about that! When I was in the Special Unit at Belmarsh, the screws only had to say they'd had an anonymous tip-off that Dave Courtney was gonna try to knobble the jury and suddenly there was an exclusion zone around them when I actually got to court. Suddenly they'd be justified in keeping armed guards with the jury at all times, making sure I was always surrounded by marksmen, and generally giving the jury more security than the social. They knew I was gonna try nothing of the sort, but they also knew how it would look to the twelve just men. 'Fuck me, he must be dangerous if we've got an armed copper in our shower with us.' You get what I'm saying? I'm pleased to report the Yank tactics are just as shit. For Gotti's trial in 1986, the prosecution actually got the judge to agree to the jury being 'impanelled'. That basically means that they're invisible to the average person in the court so they can't be intimidated by anyone in the gallery either during the case or afterwards – cos no fucker knows what they looked like. Where Gotti earned his gangster number one credentials was in having his people everywhere. It didn't matter to him if his jury was impanelled, imperfect or in fucking Timbuktu – he had good reason to believe he would be found Not Guilty. Sixty thousand good reasons, in fact, all of them with Abraham Lincoln's mush on.

How wicked is this? You've got half the gross national product of Mexico thrown at trying to bring down the head of the Gambino Family, and it has been suggested that a few greenbacks in the right pocket to a particularly open-minded member of the jury and the Don walks. Instead of wasting all that money fitting criminals up, you'd think the authorities would actually think about doing deals with the juries. That's what we do – guaranteed results every time!

Even though they was run by a cross-dresser, the FBI's got its reputation to think of. And when they go after you, there's none of this messing around waiting for you to do something wrong. They just bug your house till it's got more radio waves pouring out than Radio One, and then they wait for you to dig your own grave. And of course, eventually, John Gotti did that.

He had good reason to believe he would be found Not Guilty. Sixty thousand good reasons, in fact, all of them with Abraham Lincoln's mush on.

When it comes to British villains, Americans know two names: the Krays and Dave Courtney – and since the Krays don't do that many chat shows, I'm the one carrying the flag over there for British crime. **DAVE**

> The thing is, Gotti knew the police knew who he was – and what he was – they just couldn't prove it. And what a dreamy feeling that is.

Like all the classic Dons though, Gotti rose through the ranks of the Gambino Family by arranging little accidents for the bloke just ahead of him. 'Mind that bullet. Oh, too late. Still, better luck next time…' And it didn't hurt his reputation when he was sent to take out the murderer of Carlo Gambino's son. What a rush is that? Being asked to do a personal hit by the then Don himself.

What makes him a good role model for the criminal fraternity is the fact he treated the 'Family' as a proper fucking unit. And, as far as he was concerned, the only way it was gonna work was if the authorities didn't know it existed. You with me? According to the official papers, the boy of the Family's former number two, Armond Dellacroce, died of a 'cerebral haemorrhage brought about by chronic alcohol poisoning' shortly after pleading guilty at trial to various gangland activities. Funny coincidence that, weren't it? He mentions that the Family actually exists in court and a few days later he's got more booze in his body than blood.

The thing is, Gotti knew the police knew who he was – and what he was – they just couldn't prove it. And what a dreamy feeling that is. I'm in the same position, so I know. Because the authorities haven't really accepted I don't do crime no more, my house and my car are bugged all the time while they wait to catch me out. Every word I say is listened to, and every journey I make is logged. That knowledge would bring down a lot of people, but obviously I'm gonna have some fun with it, aren't I? There are too many people who look up to me for me to do anything else. So get this – I haven't paid a phone bill in three years – in fact I haven't even received one. If they've gone to the effort of getting a warrant to bug my gaff, they're hardly gonna let me get cut off, are they? So now I know this, I make sure I phone Australia every night – I don't even

know any fucker there, I just love the idea of it costing some police inspector a tenner from his budget just to hear this wrong number and me talking to a sheep for half an hour. (I love Australia – it's a country where the men are men, and so are the women.)

Gotti's way of sticking two fingers up at the Old Bill was to be as flashy as possible. Where have you heard that before? He'd get preferential treatment in courtrooms cos his boys would sweep the place before he stepped in. One of them would hold an umbrella over his Teflon bonce if it rained, and he even had geezers ready with the paper towels once he'd finished taking a slash. And the more police watching, the more he queened it up. And the authorities just watched this and sobbed.

Once you're the man in charge of a Family, you can't really do anything wrong because all eyes are on you. Their whole life, them Family people, they know they're on stage. The higher up you go in an organization like that, the more like businessmen you actually are than real criminals. But the police are in it for the long-term. They always say, as long as they have advanced information on what you're doing, they can fuck you. Whether it's getting a job or any other plans, they can put a spoke in the wheel and actually starve you and force you into doing other things. They can engineer it so you've got fuck all work, then they send somebody in to offer to sell you something at such a stupid price you'd be an idiot not to take it up, so they force you into taking that risk. Once you actually know that they are capable of getting a known carrier of AIDS, a prostitute, to go and shag someone on purpose and watch them die over the next five years, anything is acceptable, you know what I mean? It was the bugs that finally did for Gotti. Between 30 November 1989 and 24 January 1990, Gotti said enough on tape to bring the Family into semi-retirement for the foreseeable future, and the Teflon Don became the Velcro Don.

On my last visit to New York, I was met at the airport by one of the Gambino boys and taken to see the top chaps. Everything you imagine about Italian-American gangsters is true, and they made me a dinner I couldn't refuse. Fuck me, I've never eaten so much pasta and kissed as many blokes in my life, not sober anyway. Then, cos I had an appointment at Jay-Z's club, they drove me there.

They might not be known too well to the authorities, but everyone on the street knows fucking well who the Family is, so when this blacked out stretch limo pulled up outside 40-40, you literally heard sphincters tighten. The geezers at the club didn't know whether I was still pissed off that Jay-Z had used one of my pictures on the cover of his album without permission, but since I was pulling up outside with the Gambinos as my chauffeur, they didn't fancy their chances if I was. That was a bit special, I will admit. Put it this way, I didn't pay to get in.

Of course, the truth is, when you've got the top US punk band Rancid calling you 'England's Robin Hood' in one of their songs, and the biggest gangsta artist in America nicking your pictures to go on his records it's a fucking honour. I must be doing something right. What do you think?

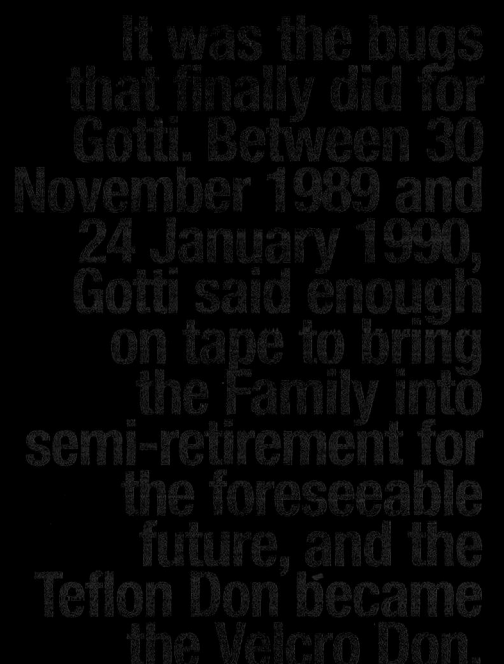

It was the bugs that finally did for Gotti. Between 30 November 1989 and 24 January 1990, Gotti said enough on tape to bring the Family into semi-retirement for the foreseeable future, and the Teflon Don became the Velcro Don.

AND THE LINK IS…

I've become close to the Family in the last few years thanks to a mate of mine called Wilf Pine, the 'gentleman gangster in New York'. Because I intend to make America my home eventually, Wilf spread the word so that every time I go to the States, I'm chuffed as fuck to find I've got the Gambinos as my tour guides!

Bruce Reynolds
Call Me Ishmael

FACTS
BRUCE REYNOLDS
CALL ME ISHMAEL

DAVE'S DODGY DOSSIER

The Daily Mail likes to think of itself as the paper for law and order, but it was working in their offices as a teenager that drove Bruce Reynolds into dreaming of a life of crime to escape the monotony. After a series of smaller crimes and various spells inside, Bruce hit his stride as a safe-cracker and lived the playboy life of Cary Grant in To Catch a Thief, flitting between the South of France and England. Most famously he was the mastermind of the Great Train Robbery – the job he describes as the Sistine Chapel or the Moby Dick of his career.

HIS DODGIEST DAY

It might have been the one that did for him, but Bruce Reynolds and the Great Train Robbery go hand in hand, don't they? It's Luke Skywalker v Darth Vader, Churchill v Hitler, Che Guevara v the whole of fucking America. You know it's out there, you know it might beat you, but you've got to have a go. Come on!

> **He planned everything down to the last detail and made sure everyone was trained to do the little job he had for them.**

Bruce Reynolds is someone I've got an awful lot of time and respect for. He's a real, proper gentleman. He gives off an air of major royalty around him. You're honoured in his company and you feel that. Christ, what the fuck's he doing in the Villains section?

He was the brains behind the Great Train Robbery, which has gone down in history as one of the most famous jobs ever. They've made films about it, for fuck's sake. You don't get more famous than that. And Bruce has gone down in history as one of the business's smart men, cos he really was what we used to call a criminal mastermind. He's a naughty boy, make no mistake, but he's not a fighty gangster or anything like that. He knows what he's good at and it's thinking.

Back in the days when you'd do jobs like military operations, he planned everything down to the last detail and made sure everyone was trained to do the little job he had for them. That bloke would carry the shooter, that bloke would get the locks open, that bloke would drive the car. And Bruce would be the geezer pulling the strings like Michael Caine in The Italian Job. (I actually think old Mike modelled himself a bit on Bruce – and not a lot of people know that.)

He calls the Great Train Robbery his Moby Dick (even that's a bit literary). 'I went after the one big one and the one big one I went after actually killed me.' Well, call me fucking Ishmael. When you're a thinker, you need challenges. A normal little thief will just steal from one day to the next cos that's what he does. Drivers drive, dogs bark, thieves nick. Them's the rules. You get opportunist villains who see an open window and take that as an invite to pop in. And you get ones who plan to do a certain gaff but they don't really know what they'll find inside. But people like Bruce look around for a target worthy of their talents and then they go, 'What do I have to do to make this work?'

> *Cos of how he was and how he lived, he was the wrong age to get a bit of bird, weren't he? I think it probably affected him more than a lot of other people.* **DAVE**

Most criminals would be happy knowing the amount of money they'd be divvying up at the end of the night. For your actual mastermind like Bruce, he wants to know that he's beaten this thing that's supposedly unbeatable. For him it's the David and Goliath thing, it's about the satisfaction of taking on an opponent who's bigger than him and pissing all over him. And the Great Train Robbery was one of those mythical targets that you'd dream about. Like Fort Knox in America or the Bank of England – it's one of the Holy Grails of villainy. And he went for it.

What happened next is all a bit sad, in my opinion. Cos of how he was and how he lived, he was the wrong age to get a bit of bird, weren't he? I think it probably affected him more than a lot of other people.

Because he's smart, Bruce Reynolds has not surrounded himself with loads of other old villains. His wife ain't very well and he's dedicated his life to looking after her and keeping away from the one thing which might fucking egg him back into crime – which is other fucking villains! If you ain't in the business, it's hard to explain. But you get a few of the chaps together and the old cogs start whirring over a few jars and suddenly you're planning a raid on Cherie Blair's lipstick collection for a laugh. And cos Bruce loves nothing more than a challenge, that's the worst thing that can happen to him. He needs to be kept too busy to wonder 'what if…?'

These days Bruce is based in Clerkenwell in London and is very active in the running of a place called Tardis, along with his son and a bloke called George. It's a wicked little venue. I've had book launches there and my head once appeared there as part of an exhibition called 'From Cons to Icons'. His boy Nick is a fantastically talented artist and sculptor, and he made busts (I thought it was just the Old Bill that done that) of all the chaps' heads: you had me, Ronnie Biggs, his old man, Freddie Foreman, Frankie Fraser. It nearly went tits up though, cos the night before the opening some cunt run off with my head! You've got to be a fucking sandwich short of a picnic to pull a stunt like that, haven't you? And I think the geezer who done it realized this as soon as his pants started turning a different colour on the way home.

He actually sent a taxi back with the head on the back seat which fucking freaked the cabbie, and a note that said, 'Sorry, Dave, I never meant to nick your head – I thought it was Ronnie Biggs!' Well hit me with a shovel and call me Dug. I don't know what's worse – not being good enough to be nicked or being mistaken for a geezer who's a foot shorter and about thirty years older than me. Prick. Anyway, Nick plays harmonica in a band called the Alabama 3 and his girlfriend is also a singer with them. He was actually a special Navy Seal before he retired so he's got some stories. I just hope they don't fire the old man up too much.

> **If you ain't in the business, it's hard to explain. But you get a few of the chaps together and the old cogs start whirring over a few jars and suddenly you're planning a raid on Cherie Blair's lipstick collection for a laugh.**

The Great Train Robbery was one of those mythical targets that you'd dream about. Like Fort Knox in America or the Bank of England.

AND THE LINK IS...
Bruce and I meet up so we can talk about the cricket, the weather, the foreign secretary's stand on the Rhodesia problem - shut the fuck up! Normally we just talk about our books. His is a fucking encyclopaedia, I promise you.

VILLAIN

Roy 'Pretty Boy' Shaw & Lenny 'The Guv'nor' McLean
Bruise Company

FACTS
ROY 'PRETTY BOY' SHAW & LENNY 'THE GUV'NOR' McLEAN BRUISE COMPANY

DAVE'S DODGY DOSSIER
Lenny and Roy are legends of the bare-knuckle boxing game. One bloke didn't know the meaning of pain. The other one didn't know the meaning of small. And neither of them knew the meaning of antidisestablishmentarianism. At a time when unlicensed boxing was as closely associated with gangsters as spats and violin cases, these two were the giants of the sport. Literally, in Lenny's case. Very possibly the scariest men who ever lived.

THEIR DODGIEST DAY
Three tear-ups in front of thousands of people in Finsbury Park. One each, then Roy won the decider. Talk about the unstoppable force meets the immovable object. It's U.S.A. v Russia, Bond v Blofeld, Godzilla v King Kong, Take That v fucking Boyzone. With knobs on.

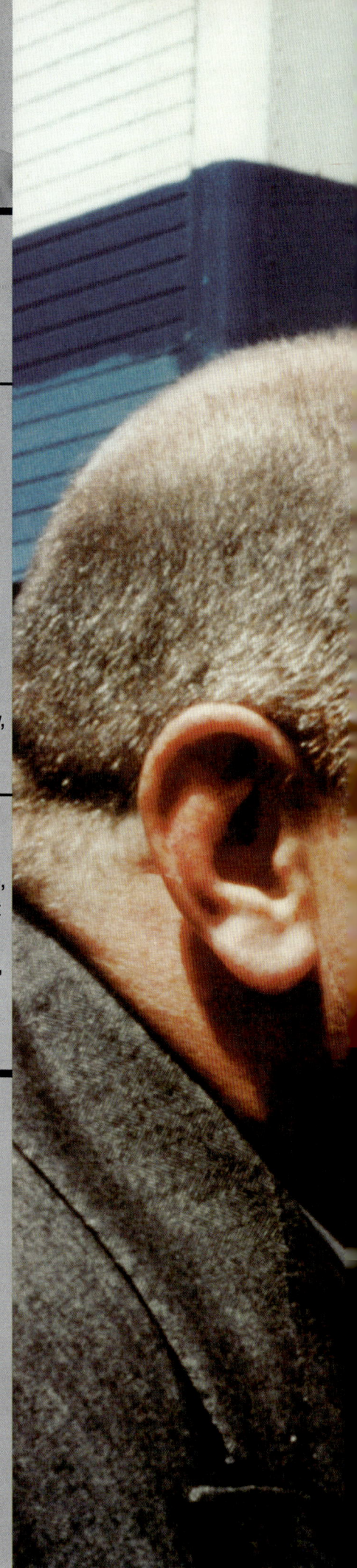

These two fucking hated each other but they had some memorable 'What were you doing the night Roy and Lenny went at it?' fights so it seems fitting to talk about them together. Let's see if something kicks off.

Roy Shaw was born to fight. Literally. Ever since a midwife slapped him into life and he knocked her spark out, he's never looked back. I believe he was actually put on this Earth to grab hold of another geezer and hit him till his own mum wouldn't recognize him.

But the funny thing is, Roy didn't actually get into boxing until he was 42 – before that he used to just beat geezers up for fun! And even then he'd take on all-comers – banks, building societies, security vans. Anything that had a bit of loot in it, he'd have a go. For years he held the record for the biggest armed robbery in British history (and not just cos he had the biggest arms), although he did get an eighteen stretch for his pains. I think he must have liked the food there, though, cos Roy's actually been in 22 prisons in his life – everywhere from a nuthouse in Germany to Pentonville in London (five times). That must be another fucking record, right? Let's see them stick that one on Record Breakers.

But it was when he got into the unlicensed boxing game with Joey Pyle that Roy really got noticed. I think that appealed to him, cos bare-knuckle fights was actually illegal at the time. These days it's just unlicensed by the British Boxing Board, but back then you could actually get put away just from going to watch. You could get nicked for doing it, you could get nicked for conspiracy to murder just for putting the show on. But there's always something sexy about being somewhere that could get raided by the police, ain't there? Whether it's a boxing match to the death or one of those fucking great raves I used to put on on the M25. It's half the attraction.
There was a load of other superstars in the game at the time as well as Roy and Lenny, but they didn't actually get the publicity they deserved cos they was behind these two giants all the time. But there was Harry Starbuck, Columbo, Cliff 'Iron Man' Fields, Teddy Webb, Fred the Head, Donnie 'The Bull' Adams, dozens of them. All great, great fighters.

The thing about Roy, though, is that pound for pound he was probably the hardest cunt of the lot. I can't see anyone going with Roy Shaw. It's a bit like this: you know with some dogs you can pick up a roll of paper and before you hit it the bastard's run off whimpering. But other dogs can hang off a moving tyre for a day and if you kick it up the bollocks it goes, 'Thank you.' Roy's the human equivalent of one of them. Not only has he got more punch than your average suburban drinks party, he don't seem to feel the pain he fucking should do. He's like one of those cartoons where you smack a bloke a thousand times and then he just picks the geezer up and twats him once. An awesome, awesome man.

Even though he's had more porridge than Goldilocks, Roy don't regret doing the things he has just cos 99 people out of 100 would have done something different. His take on life is just 'Well, it's what I do, innit?' But he's a proper success story as well, cos a few years ago he bought his missus some land to graze her horses on. Then the government comes along and gives him millions so they can build on it. Fucking touch! And he deserves it, cos he's fucking wicked.

Three of the greatest nights of my life was when I went to see Roy go flat-nose to flat-nose with Lenny McLean. I actually paid to go and see these two hit shit out of each other every time they got together, and I weren't alone. Every hardnut, gangster, wannabe and celebrity seemed to be at Finsbury Park when these two got together. It was actually scary. Armageddon unleashed in a fucking boxing ring. But the good news is it made me realize that I should retire from the sport. Quick.

Lenny McLean was one of the most awesome things I've seen in full flight. He was already doing it in the ring when I started out boxing and without any shadow of a doubt he was someone I looked up to. **DAVE**

Them two were legends. Every gangster knew about them, they was part of folklore, even though Lenny weren't a gangster himself. He'd been a window cleaner and a bouncer and eventually he came and worked with me as a doorman and a debt collector. You think you've got problems with Dave Courtney standing outside your door? Take a look up and that wall you thought I was standing in front of is actually a bloke. And he wants to hit you if you don't give back what you owe, thank you very much. (He got a part in Lock, Stock and Two Smoking Barrels just being how he was – I should have been up there with him, but it was blocked by the authorities.)

Even though I've seen him as a boxer, I was more impressed by what Lenny could do as a fighting doorman. I come from an era where doormen were a lot different to what they are now and one of the most memorable sights in my life is Lenny McLean as the picture book doorman standing there like a Christmas tree with dozens of blokes hanging off him, all of them snarling and growling and he's swatting them off. It's purely down to his size but that don't make it less impressive.

Because he was built like Giant Haystacks' big brother, Lenny McLean was one of the most awesome things I've seen in full flight. He was already doing it in the ring when I started out boxing and without any shadow of a doubt he was someone I looked up to. But he did have an awful lot of nature on his side, being six foot eight and 22 stone. So by the time he started sticking all these injections up his arse to get even heavier and make him a little bit more short-tempered, you was in a bit of fucking trouble if the cunt was out there with the hump.

I've said already that I think Roy Shaw was the tastiest bastard going, and probably still is, but there is no sight scarier than 22 stone of Lenny McLean running at you from the other side of the ring. And I know cos I was fucking stupid enough to spar with him once. What a prick, what the fuck was I doing? We was at the Thomas à Beckett gym and I lasted about 30 seconds, which was about the time it took Len to get out of his chair and reach me. He just belted across the ring going 'Yaaaaaaaaagh!' and even though I've put my hands up in a cross in front of me (for protection, I weren't praying yet), he's hit the first one so hard it's smashed into the second one which smacked me in my own face and knocked me out. 'Thanks for the workout, Dave…'

Cos we worked together on and off for fifteen years, I've been out with Lenny loads of times. And that gets you noticed. It's the same with Roy Shaw. We go out a lot and have a good time, particularly at Epping Forest Country Club and people just want to come and have a chat. He's a celebrity and a bit of a hero where he lives in Essex and I have to say he handles it like he handles anything, which is blinding.

But when Lenny got a taste of this fame thing, through his book The Guv'nor and the film, that changed him a little bit. He was a much nicer bloke before all that. And his dying was a bit messy, cos he saw when he was on his last legs and he tried very hard to make sure he was immortalized somehow, in books, films, interviews, anything really. And that actually made him do some naughty things like borrow money off people for a film that never came out, with me being one of them people. Fifteen grand from me, Johnny Jacket gave ten, and so did a load of others. And all of a sudden it was, 'I'm dying of cancer and I can't come out and I don't want to be seen by anyone. I'm just in bed and I'm six stone.' So you couldn't even ask for your money back, fucking cheeky cunt. It's sad, but Lenny actually left on quite a sore note for a lot of people. He was a very funny cunt and I liked the geezer a lot, he was a good friend to me. But near the end he was a bit guilty of being a bully and I saw him take liberties with a few people and push his luck a bit more than he should have done. But good luck on you, Len. See you soon.

> **I think Roy Shaw was the tastiest bastard going, and probably still is, but there is no sight scarier than 22 stone of Lenny McLean running at you from the other side of the ring.**

Them two were legends. Every gangster knew about them, they was part of folklore.

AND THE LINK IS...
Cos we worked together on and off for 15 years, I've been out with Lenny loads of times. And that gets you noticed. It's the same with Roy Shaw. He's a celebrity and a bit of a hero where he lives in Essex and I have to say he handles it like he handles anything, which is blinding.

VILLAIN

Freddie Foreman
The Managing Director of British Crime

FACTS

FREDDIE FOREMAN MANAGING DIRECTOR OF BRITISH CRIME

DAVE'S DODGY DOSSIER

Freddie Foreman was a boy to make any dad proud. His family didn't like the authorities, so Fred didn't neither. No questions asked. He had a colourful childhood and kept out of trouble for years, until his first court case for GBH at the grand old age of sixteen. Freddie earned and thoroughly deserved his reputation as a villain and a hard bastard. If you wanted problems taken care of, Fred was your man. If you happened to drive a security truck with loads of wonga inside, bad luck – cos Fred was probably coming after you.

HIS DODGIEST DAY

The old double jeopardy law coming in, that means you can now be tried for the same crime more than once, is gonna give us more of this, but when Freddie happened to mention the true story of Frank Mitchell's mysterious disappearance in one of his books, the Old Bill got interested and nicked him for it. Bastards.

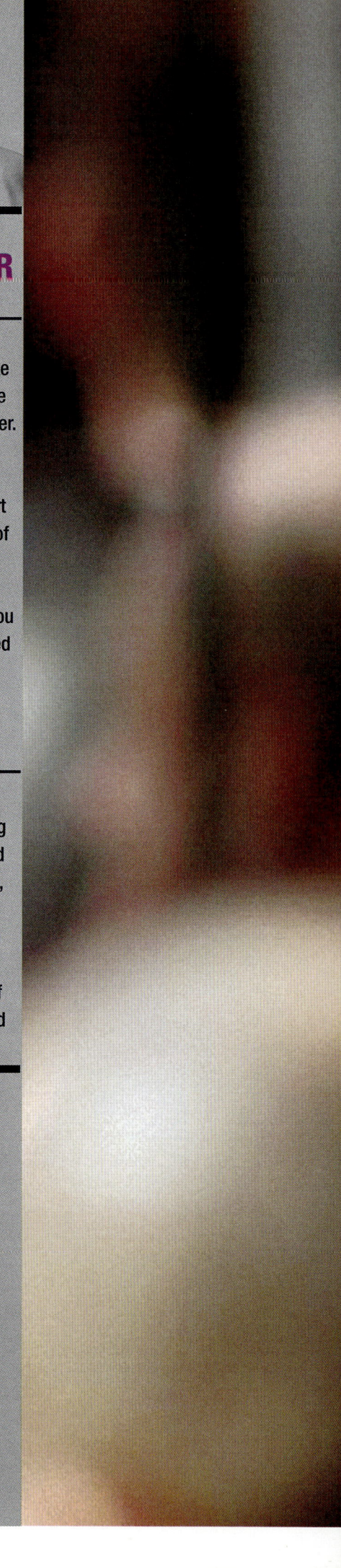

DAVE'S DUSTER-O-METER
INFLUENCE 4
LEADERSHIP 5
SUCCESS 4
NAUGHTINESS 4
MYTHOLOGY 4

He worked in a time when there was a code among villains and he brought a bit of dignity to the profession. **DAVE**

He had
of th
he had n
the Rich
no fear o

No fear of the Krays, no fear of the Richardsons, no fear of anyone.

Every page you turn in the British crime history books will have this gentleman's fingerprints all over them – and not just cos he nicked the fucking book in the first place.

Freddie Foreman is called The Managing Director of British Crime and The Undertaker – both nicknames he not only richly deserves, but he earned. He's classic old school, ain't he? He worked in a time when there was a code among villains and he brought a bit of dignity to the profession. Nothing he did was cos he was in a bad mood or you caught him at a bad time. He was a professional man and all the naughty stuff he did was just business. But what a fucking business!

Freddie operated south of the river and he had his own little firm. I think the Great Train Robber Buster Edwards was actually part of his outfit. He was a very, very naughty bit of work was Freddie Foreman and the other firms just let him get on with it. When Ronnie Kray died, Freddie was actually one of the four pallbearers – he represented the South, Charlie Kray was there for the East, Teddy Dennis was West and Johnny Nash held the end up for the North. He had no fear of the Krays, he had no fear of the Richardsons, no fear of anyone.

He was called The Undertaker for obvious reasons, but for the hard of thinking, I'll tell you anyway – he made people disappear. If they were alive, he could put a stop to that. And if they weren't, he could lose them for other people. If you want to split hairs he was more interested in the crematorium side of things than burials, if you know what I mean, but the end result was the same – a load of coppers holding the A to Z scratching their heads.

Fred had his own pub and people went down in that pub cellar and never came out. And who says drinking isn't dangerous for your health? The reason a lot of people know his name today is cos of one body in particular that he helped go missing.

Reggie Kray was gonna kill someone at a party. His name was Jack 'The Hat' McVitie – ringing any bells yet? Reg nearly cocks it up but he finally chops the bloke to bits with the pub's cutlery, then they have to get rid of the body. So the twins get the junior of the firm to take care of it. And that was Tony Lambrianou. He's the fresh-faced, eager to please kid who, cos he's starting out and wants to make a name for himself, probably does a few jobs that aren't that clever. 'All right,' he goes, 'give it to me.' But Tony really didn't have a fucking clue what to do, so he rings his bruv. Chris Lambrianou comes round and says, 'I don't know what to do – we'll ring Freddie Foreman.' Freddie says, 'All right, get it through the Blackwall Tunnel and I'll dispose of it for you.'

So that's what happened. The Lambrianous got Jack the Hat through the pipe and Freddie Foreman had one of his famous barbecues. As far as anyone at the party is concerned, Tony and Chris dumped the stiff, so when they all got captured and asked who lost the body, they all said, 'Tony Lambrianou.' Cos there was no body and they might find that a stumbling block in the court case, the police went to Tony, 'Tell me where the body is – I know you had nothing to do with the murder – and you can walk.' And his answer was, 'I can't.' So he got famous for being Mr Silent, the staunch geezer for not telling anybody, but in reality he couldn't tell them where the body was cos he didn't have a fucking clue. And he couldn't say he gave it to Fred, neither, cos Fred is not the type of person to drop in it.

Here's another one from Freddie's scrapbook that you might have heard of cos again it involved another cock-up by the Krays. When their boy Frank Mitchell got busted, the twins decided they would break him out. They had no reason to, but then they never had a reason for half the fucking things they did. In actual fact, Mitchell managed to hop over the wall himself and all Reg and Ron did was sit there in the car park with the engine running. But guess who took all the credit for masterminding it? Got it in one.

You could stand on the steps of the Old Bailey and go, 'I done it' a dozen times and no one could touch you – I know that for a fact, cos I did every time. **DAVE**

Cos they never thought it through, they're now stuck with a bloke on the run who can't work cos he might be recognized, so they have to support him. So this is where another call to Freddie comes in. On the day that Mitchell stopped breathing, you couldn't honestly say Freddie Foreman had the tightest of alibis, but a court found him Not Guilty and the official reason for death was put down as sunstroke or something like that. But then Freddie made the mistake of 'fessing all in his autobiography Respect. And the shit's really hit then.

At the 2005 general election, the Conservative party actually promised to stop villains like me and Fred earning a crust from writing books about our criminal past – and I reckon they lost hundreds of thousands of votes because of that. Some of those votes, I bet, came from the Old Bill cos without these books they wouldn't have a fucking clue what goes on. So the authorities are actually bringing in this double jeopardy law that says you can now be tried for the same thing twice. Before, if you got Not Guilty, that was the end of it. You could stand on the steps of the Old Bailey and go, 'I done it' a dozen times and no one could touch you – I know that for a fact, cos I did every time. With the new law, they can have another pop at you. So cos he re-opened the Mitchell can of worms (and that's probably all that was left of him anyway), Freddie actually got himself into trouble later on. At the time he was living the dream in Marbella and they got him quite late, which I thought was bang out of order. But it never changed him.

Freddie was as real as you can get and is still a very scary man today. He looks as lovely as any other 70-year-old and he is truly a very nice man and a good friend, but I should imagine he's got the scariest Filofax in the world. Even though he's very straight today, if need be he could make a phone call that would fuck up your life big time.

Freddie was a proper bit of work, a very good, true testosterony man. He could proper handle himself in other words. And even today, although he looks like he wouldn't say boo to a goose, I can happily report he's still got it. A couple of years ago, Sad Frankie Fraser had been spreading the word that a couple of people were grasses. One of them was me – but what silly old gits like him say about me I don't care. The other one was Freddie Foreman, which is a big mistake however old you are. So when Fred saw Frank in a café in Maida Vale, he went for him. Actually fucking went for him, smashed him to the ground and gave him a slap like he hadn't had for thirty years. I imagine reading about it must be quite funny, these two old grave dodgers with a combined age of 145 having a proper tear up in a west London café, but if you saw Frank afterwards you knew it weren't a laugh. Like the man's book says, Respect.

He looks as lovely as any other 70-year-old and he is truly a very nice man and a good friend, but I should imagine he's got the scariest Filofax in the world.

I imagine reading about it must be quite funny, these two old grave dodgers with a combined age of 145 having a proper tear up in a west London cafe.

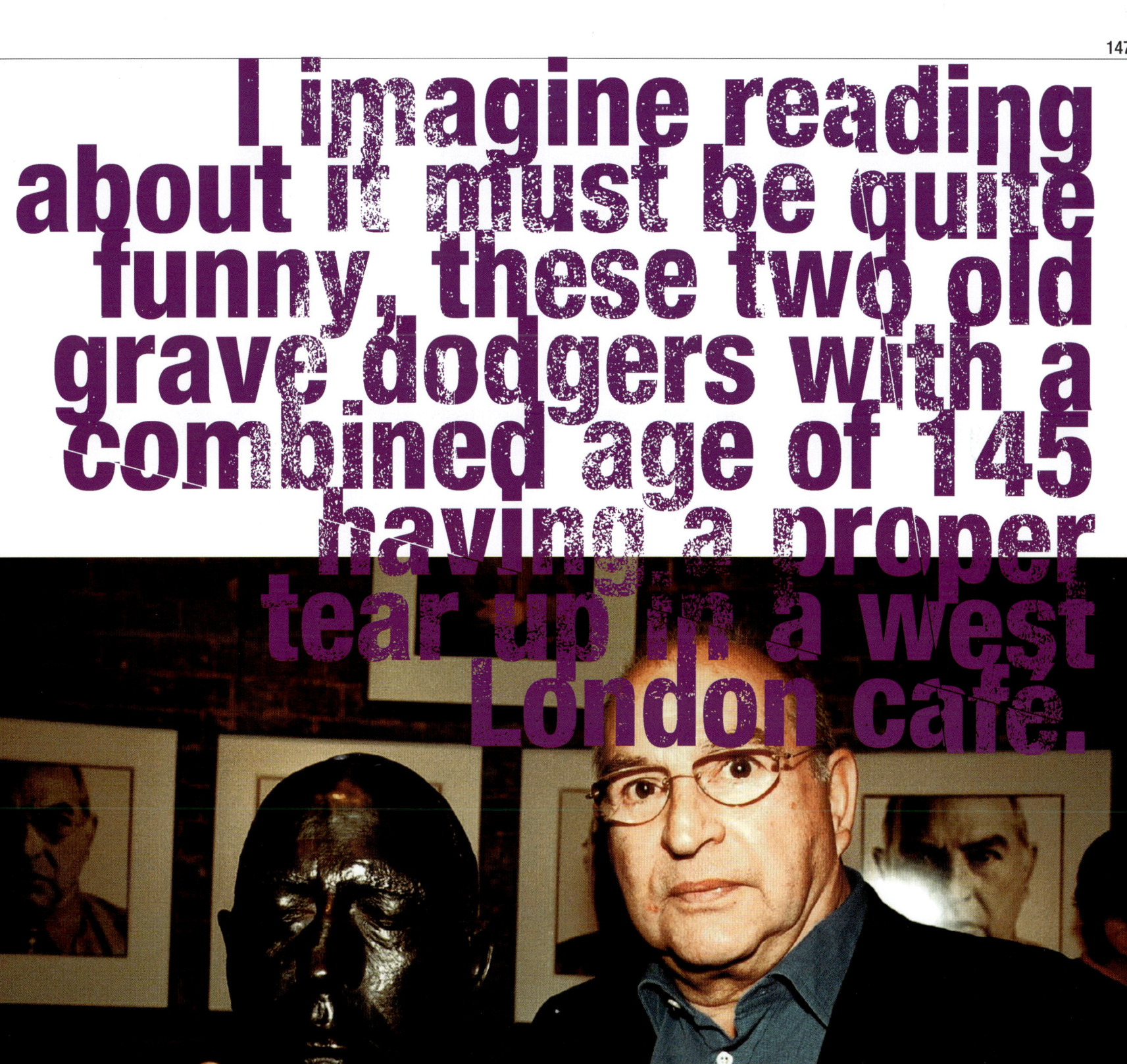

AND THE LINK IS…
Freddie was as mad as you can get and is still a very scary man today. He looks as lovely as any other 70-year-old and he is truly a very nice man and a good friend, but I should imagine he's got the scariest filofax in the world. Even though he's very straight today, if need be he could make a phone call that would fuck up your life big time.

Charles Bronson
One Flew Over The Budgie's Nest

FACTS
CHARLES BRONSON ONE FLEW OVER THE BUDGIE'S NEST

DAVE'S DODGY DOSSIER
Charles Bronson has spent the last 30 years in prisons and asylums, 26 of them in solitary confinement with just his painting apparatus and a radio for company. His reputation as a serial hostage-taker, armed robber and all-round hardnut have seen him recaptured within weeks of each release he has earned in that time. He became famous for holding rooftop protests in several of his prisons and when he changed his name to 'Charles Bronson' in 1987, the media instantly discovered a new anti-hero.

HIS DODGIEST DAY
Where do you start? But my favourite is still this one: Charlie asked every day for two years if he could have a budgie, then on the day they gave it to him he bit its head off. Fucking mental, ain't it? Imagine what went through all those screws' minds that day. 'Er, Guv, can I have a transfer?'

DAVE'S DUSTER-O-METER
INFLUENCE 1
LEADERSHIP 1
SUCCESS 1
NAUGHTINESS 5
MYTHOLOGY 5

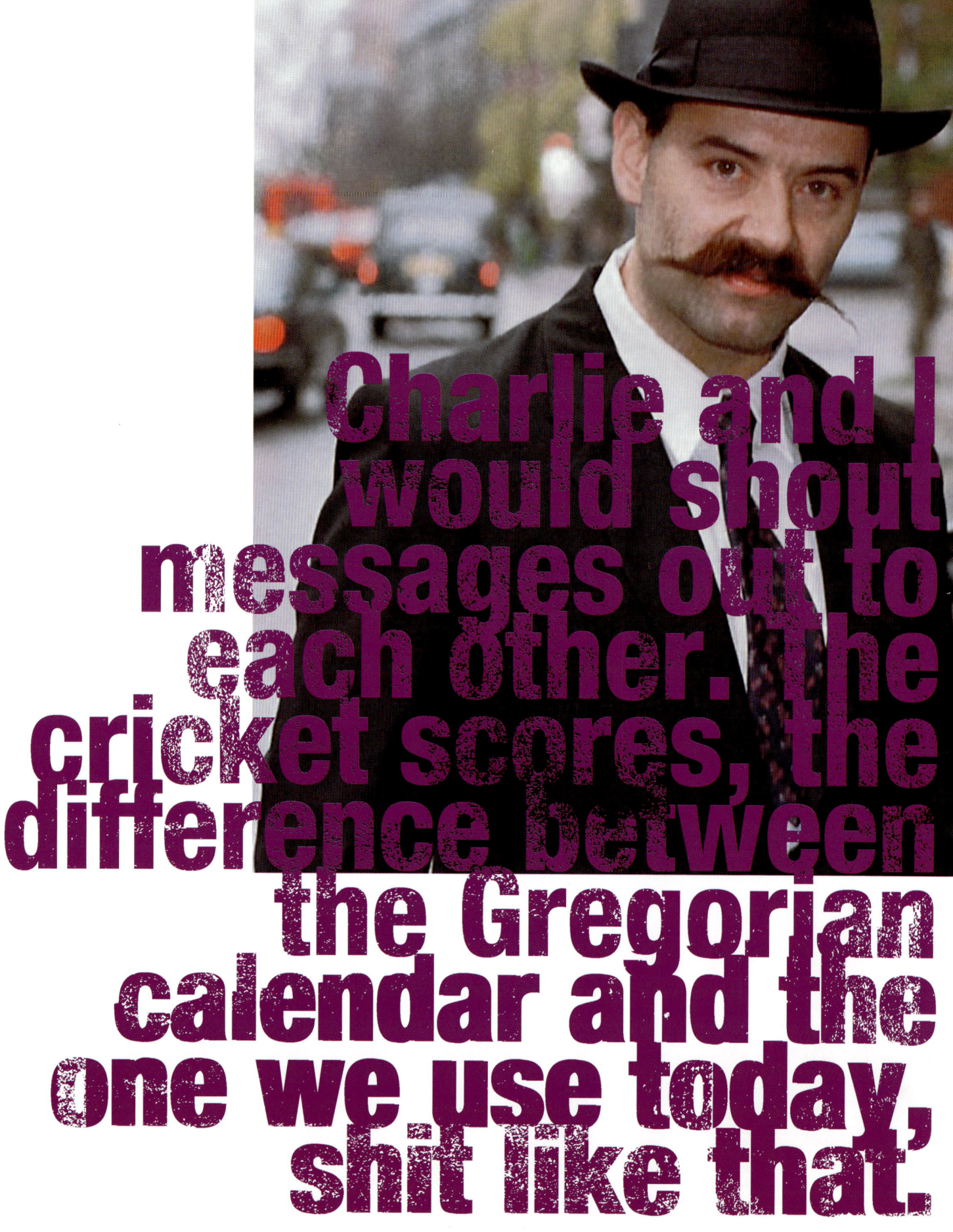

'Charlie and I would shout messages out to each other. The cricket scores, the difference between the Gregorian calendar and the one we use today, shit like that.'

> *I was kept in the Special Unit in Belmarsh and my room was directly above his cell, so I heard all the fights they had down there and all the grief he used to cause the screws.* **DAVE**

Now here's a complex character. My hat goes off to any man who can spend 26 years in solitary confinement and still have marbles mostly intact.

I actually know Charlie Bronson better than a lot of people, cos for a while I was kept in the Special Unit in Belmarsh and my room was directly above his cell, so I heard all the fights they had down there and all the grief he used to cause the screws. Obviously I weren't feeling on top of the world, ma, when they first stuck me in there and slammed the door, but somehow Charlie had heard it was me cos the next thing I hear is, 'COURTNEY!' being screamed out from the floorboards. Fucking unreal, that was! And what a welcome to the biggest piss-hole episode of my life.

Even though there was no windows, Charlie and I would shout messages out to each other. The cricket scores, the difference between the Gregorian calendar and the one we use today, shit like that. So we actually got quite tight – well, as tight as you can get with six feet of solid concrete and fourteen men with machine guns and stun rods between you.

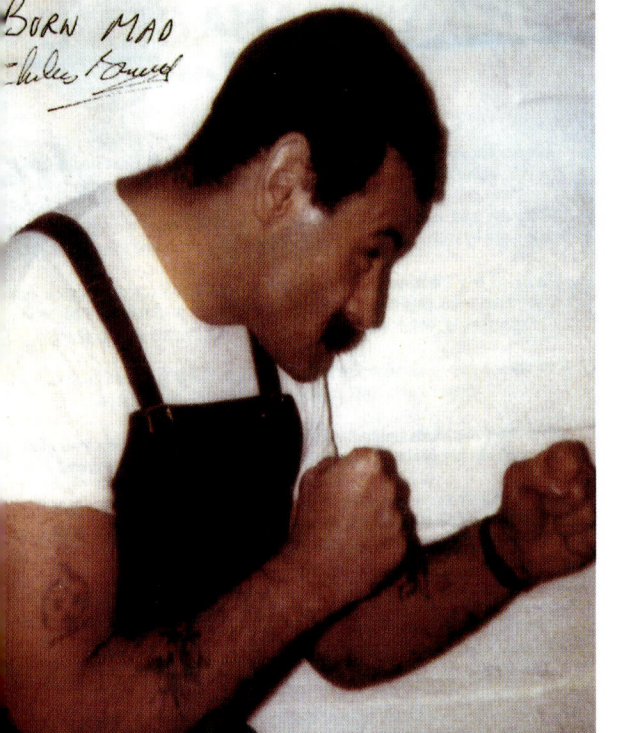

Charlie's a bit like Frankie Fraser cos although they've both served about eight hundred years, it ain't all been in one go. With Frankie, every time he's got out he's been so clueless at his next job he's been hoiked back in again. I'm sorry, but I can't respect any cunt who got caught at everything he ever did.

But with Charlie you figure there's something else going on. It's like he wants to be caught. I think in a hundred years' time we might find he was acting on orders from some alien planet or foreign government cos his behaviour totally dumbfounds any normal human instinct. Look, they let him out in 1992 – he lasted 55 days then got reeled back in on GBH, having an offensive weapon and conspiracy to rob. Dozy fucks let him out on bail, so he took a hostage. He's had hunger strikes, he's spent more time on prison roofs than the fucking pigeons, and if there's a screw to be nutted, you know he's the man for the job.

The thing with Charlie, in my opinion, is he got addicted to the buzz of being famous. The worst feeling in the world when you're inside is knowing that the outside world is still spinning and people are getting on with their lives without you. Your missus might be the best diamond in the world, but when you're inside with just your thoughts for company, you even manage to twist how good she is. Eventually you get resentful that she's having a normal life trying to support your kids. 'What, she goes to work every day? Slut!' You understand what I mean? So one day Charlie lucked on to a way to make people outside notice him. And since then he's been clocking up the attention points like a man on a mission.

Don't get me wrong, I am not knocking the man. I would call him a mate and in fact he sent me the letter to take to Ronnie Biggs' 70th birthday party (see page 164). And we correspond all the time anyway, although cos I've done bird in the Special Unit they won't let me visit him – too much of a security risk, apparently. And I was the one he asked to organize his wedding to the Pakistani bird Saira – although I'm hoping he's gonna forget that one considering how it ended up. She proper shafted him and has just written this book hanging him out to dry. She fucking destroyed him in it, according to the bits I've seen. I don't suppose she's said too many compliments about me in it, neither, which is a bit rich considering I stumped up for her fucking wedding and supplied a premier division guest list. Maybe she didn't like the vol au vents.

Here's a funny thing though. Cos she was Muslim, she couldn't marry outside her faith. She didn't have a problem marrying a fully paid up, card-carrying scary bastard murderer, but she drew the line at C of E. So Charlie, bless his romantic soul, he turned Muslim to please her. That was on the Saturday. Three days later, two jumbo jets did emergency stops inside the Twin Towers in America and suddenly the whole fucking world hates Muslims. For the first time in his life, I think Charlie was actually a bit grateful for being in solitary.

One thing came out of that wedding, though, and it weren't first night nerves – I think the honeymoon suite at Belmarsh was being cleaned at the time. At the wedding reception was Lord Longford, an amazing old geezer who even though he is firmly in with the Establishment actually devotes his whole life to helping out victims of the authorities. One of his pet projects is Charlie Bronson, so that's why he was there, but he also had a few words for me. He took me over behind the wedding cake (which had a little plastic Charlie and Saira handcuffed together on a prison roof on the top tier) and said, 'Whatever it is the authorities think about you, it goes right to the very top.' How fucking awesome is that? I knew I was causing a few ripples in high places, but this proper fucking Lord had admitted I was a one-man tsunami raging through the heart of the Establishment. Thank you, God!

But if you're gonna go raging anywhere, what better chap to have at your side than Charlie Bronson. I'm all for a bit of hand on the heart comradeship, but this geezer's code of honour takes it to a new level. All prisoners are black and white people – they're good, screws are bad. We hate them; they hate us. Them's the rules. End of. And Charlie proper lives his life like that. If you was a prisoner and he saw you getting it from a screw, he would run over and help even if you was in the wrong and even if

stupid or a bit weird and all that. Cos he happens to be a bald geezer with a bigger beard than all of ZZ Top put together, they do petty things like release pictures of him to the press all the time and say, 'Look how scary this man is.' He might be eating his All-Bran at the time, but they give it a spin and the newspaper people help them out. But it don't stop there. When he was up for appeal last time, the screws arranged it so they took him down on 1 April. They made out he was gonna get let out and they was all stomping around saying how shit that would be so he'd get his hopes up, then when the review board said, 'Fuck off back to your cell' all the screws just went, 'April Fool!' Wankers. They do loads of things like that.

As far as I'm concerned, Charlie Bronson is an absolute god of an inmate when you're looking from the outside. From the inside I imagine you'd be thanking the Lord every day for the invention of firearms, cos he's one scary muthafucker. Look, every other day he does 10,000 sit-ups. All the days in between, he does 10,000 press-ups. Talk about a six pack – you could smash and grab your local Barclays with his stomach.

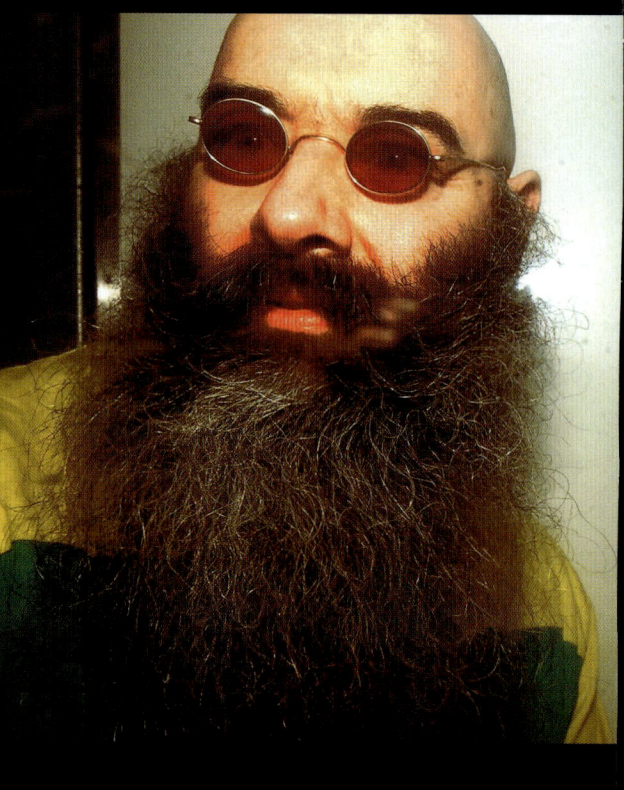

If you was a prisoner and he saw you getting it from a screw, he would run over and help even if you was in the wrong.

Charlie Bronson is an absolute god of an inmate when you're looking from the outside.

I don't know if he'll ever get out. But as long as he keeps painting and writing and we see his words and pictures in books and newspapers, I know that Charlie will be having a hard-on 24/7. And the more I get to know him, the more important I think all that is to him. He's one in a million is Charlie Bronson. And thank fuck for that!

AND THE LINK IS...
Even though there was no windows in the Special Unit Belmarsh, Charlie and I would shout messages out to each other. The cricket scores, the difference between the Gregorian calendar and the one we use today, shit like that. So we actually got quite tight – well, as tight as you can get with six feet of solid concrete and 14 men with machine guns and stun rods between you.

VILLAIN

Howard Marks
Nice to See You

FACTS

DAVE'S DODGY DOSSIER

It's not every Oxford graduate with a degree in nuclear physics and a post-grad in philosophy that becomes what the Daily Mail called 'the most sophisticated drugs baron of all time', but Howard Marks achieved it. At the height of his career he was smuggling 30-ton consignments from Thailand and Pakistan to customers all around the world. In 1988 he was sentenced to 25 years in the US Federal Penitentiary in Indiana, the country's only Federal Death Row. He served seven years.

HIS DODGIEST DAY

Getting stung with three articulated lorries full of hash outside his gaff didn't rank as the happiest event in Howie's life, but it got him famous. 'Fucking College Boy in Haul of the Century' and all that. But because of it he's now made millions from his book Mr Nice, everyone loves him and he has a great life. Respect to the geezer.

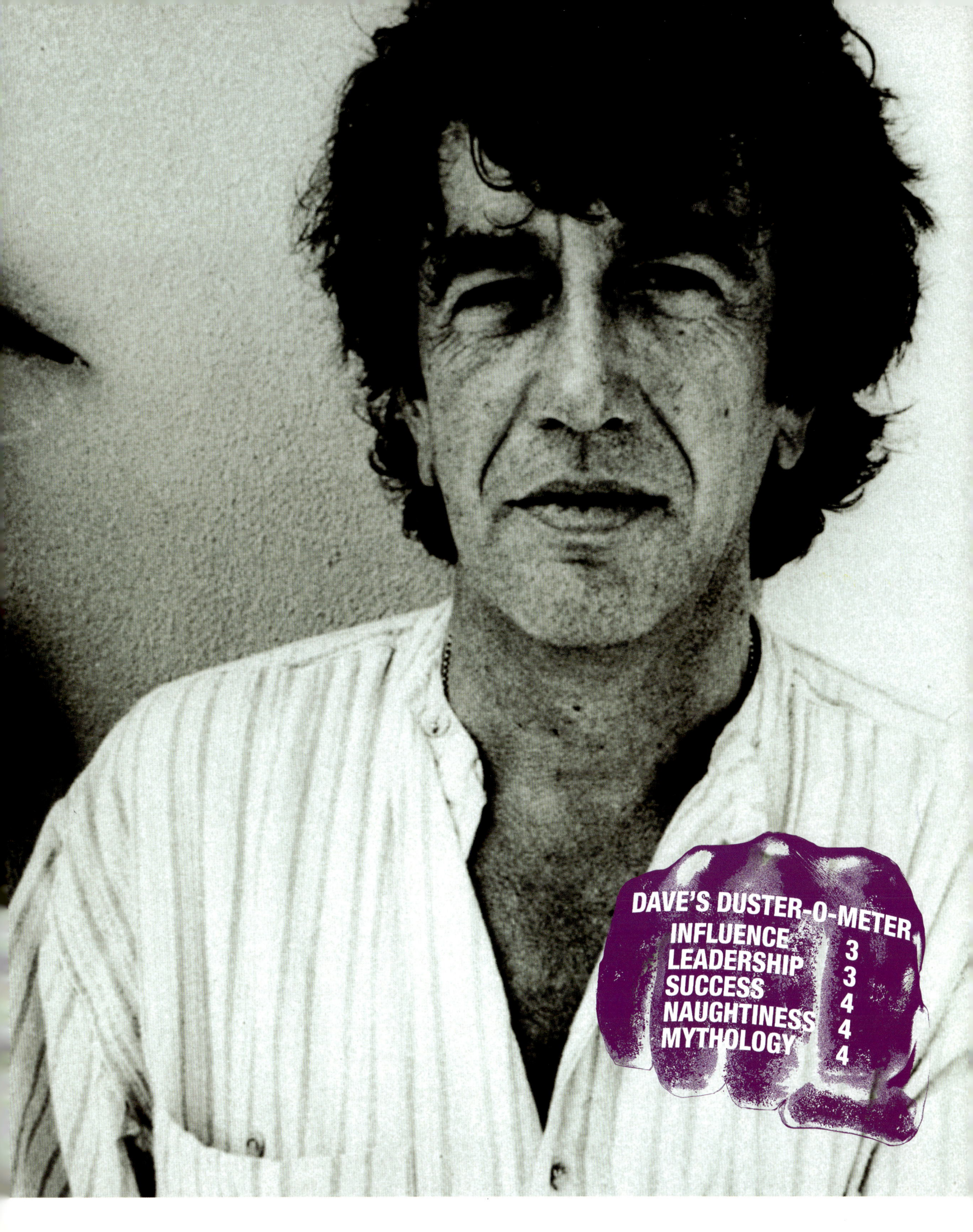

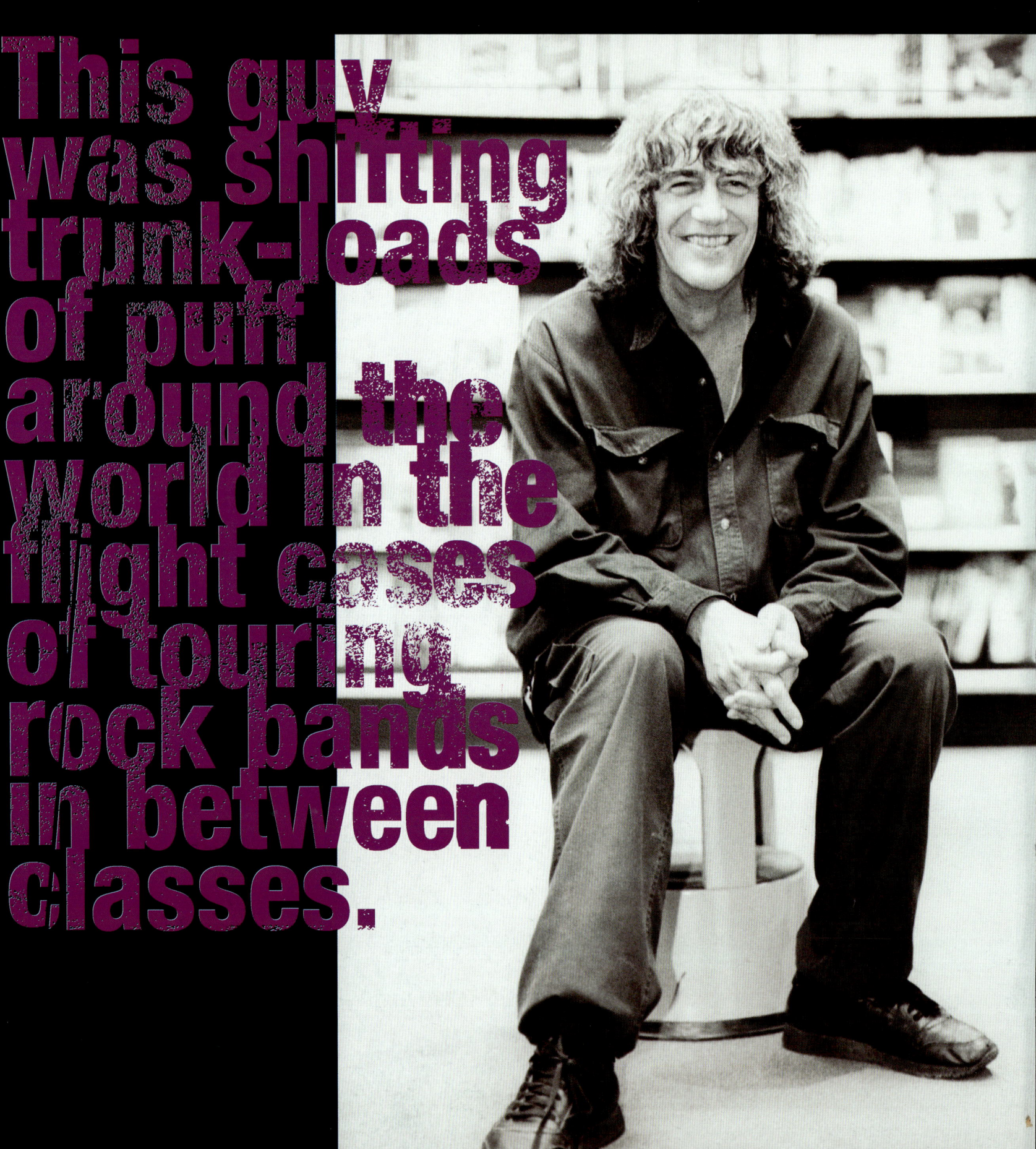

This guy was shifting trunk-loads of puff around the world in the flight cases of touring rock bands in between classes.

Not a lot of people know this, but Howard Marks is responsible for the fact that I tour the world doing Audiences With Dave Courtney – so now you know who to blame!

This is a geezer from a little Welsh mining village who happened to go to Oxford and get a degree in nuclear physics of all things, and decided that rather than blow up the world he'd try and spread a little peace, man, through hash. So some fucking respect to him for that. Most university students are signed up members of The World Owes Me A Living.Com and can't get it together to buy their own packet of fags – but this guy was shifting trunk-loads of puff around the world in the flight cases of touring rock bands in between classes. How wicked is that?

Howard Marks was in a different class. During the mid-1980s he had 43 aliases, 89 phone lines and 25 companies throughout the world. How the fuck he kept on top of all that with the amount of gear he was smoking I don't know, but he was laundering money through loads of offshore banks and bars and recording studios that he actually owned. Just running them all as legitimate businesses would have made him a multi-millionaire. But that's not the point, is it?

He became famous when he got nicked with 56 ton of puff stacked in pallets outside his house. They had aerial pictures of it being unloaded from these three fucking lorries. It was the biggest puff find the country's ever had. Cos most of the police ain't got two CSEs to rub together, they love it when they can get a college boy banged to rights, so they made a right fuss of getting hold of him, and they actually made him famous.

I was a big fan of his book Mr Nice anyway, and the fact that he was an Oxford graduate an' that appealed to me, so I paid to go and see his show at Hammersmith Odeon. And it was that night and him that made me realize my vocation was talking. I saw his show and realized, 'Wow, that is what I do all the time. I hold court – in my house, in my pub, wherever I am.' A lot of people have done worse or bigger crimes than me, but they haven't got the knack of talking about it. I can make something half-decent sound blinding. Howard Marks is just an unassuming, intelligent, witty man and he saw the funny side of everything. He saw you could disguise an awful lot of things with a joke. As long as you can laugh at something, people will enjoy listening. That's how Lock, Stock… got made. So I thought, 'As that's what I do anyway, I may as well do it on stage like him.'

I had a bit of a bond with Howard anyway, cos he had to play the grass card to get out of one of his court cases. He said, 'I was working for the CIA as an informant', knowing that, if they're asked, all they can say is 'We can't comment on that.' He knew he weren't one, but he also knew they would always refuse to comment. That was the element of doubt he needed. After he done that and got Not Guilty, that fucked them so they put him all over the papers saying 'He's a grass, he's a grass', hoping to get him shot. It's exactly the same as what they tried to do to me. In both cases, too many people knew different for it actually to work.

I can now understand why he goes around the world doing Audiences With… explaining himself after that had been said, cos I do it myself. I don't need to put my side of the story, but I do like to get it out if I can. The more people know the truth about you, the harder it is for the police to make mud stick.

It helps when you're getting your message out there if other people chip in with a bit of support, especially if they've got big audiences of their own, and that's happened to Howard and me. As soon as he got a bit of fame, the band Super Furry Animals got in touch with him and went, 'We've written a song called "Hanging Out With Howard Marks", do you

One of the highlights of my life was when I actually went on tour with him around the Canary Islands. That was fucking out of this world for me. **DAVE**

mind?' He weren't even an author then, he was just a fellow Taff and they wanted to big him up on their Fuzzy Logic album. Well the biggest punk band in America, Rancid, did the same thing with me. They actually have a track on their last album called 'Dave Courtney – England's Robin Hood' which is fucking dreamy for me cos that's how I consider myself. And so they're helping spread the word about Dave to more people than I could dream of.

Howard's a wicked geezer, absolutely superb, and, cos we've got so much in common, one of the highlights of my life was when I actually went on tour with him around the Canary Islands. That was fucking out of this world for me, cos he was the one who helped me get going as the all-singing, all-dancing Dave you know and love. I don't think even he knows this.

Not only is he fucking proper to be with, you really learn a lot of information from his shows. He's got such good little facts hidden in jokes, which is what I try to do. This is one of his tips: if you can get hold of lion's shit, which you can from London Zoo or whatever, if you're a drug dealer, all you have to do is sprinkle some of it on the front doormat of your house. And if you ever get raided by the police with their dogs, before they even walk in they smell that and go, 'There is a seventeen-stone cat in here.' No dog walking across your threshold is any use after that. He can't smell puff, Pedigree Chum or his own bollocks, cos he can't get it out of his head that he's just smelt cat shit by something that's seventeen-stone. Why would he know the difference between a lion and a cat? He's never seen a David Attenborough programme, has he?

Here's another one of Howard's, although fuck knows how he found it out. Anyway, the most potent form of LSD in the world is reindeer piss, cos their natural diet is magic mushrooms. So who knows what's going on in their little heads while they're running around? That's why they jump over things that ain't there, dodge all over the place and all that bollocks. No wonder Santa Claus gets them to pull his fucking sleigh – 'Come on, lads, let's run in the fucking sky!' Touch. So if you can actually get reindeer piss, which is fucking hard – finding a reindeer is one thing, actually running around with a jar waiting for it to have a wee is another – you have got yourself the most potent form of LSD there is. And don't ask me who discovered that. Or how they discovered that.

Howard's full of them, little facts like that. He can tell you how to get high on certain toads if you give them a lick and make you crack up with laughter, but he's still getting his messages across: I ain't a grass, drugs should be legal, the Old Bill are wankers. What a legend. And I am a very, very big fan.

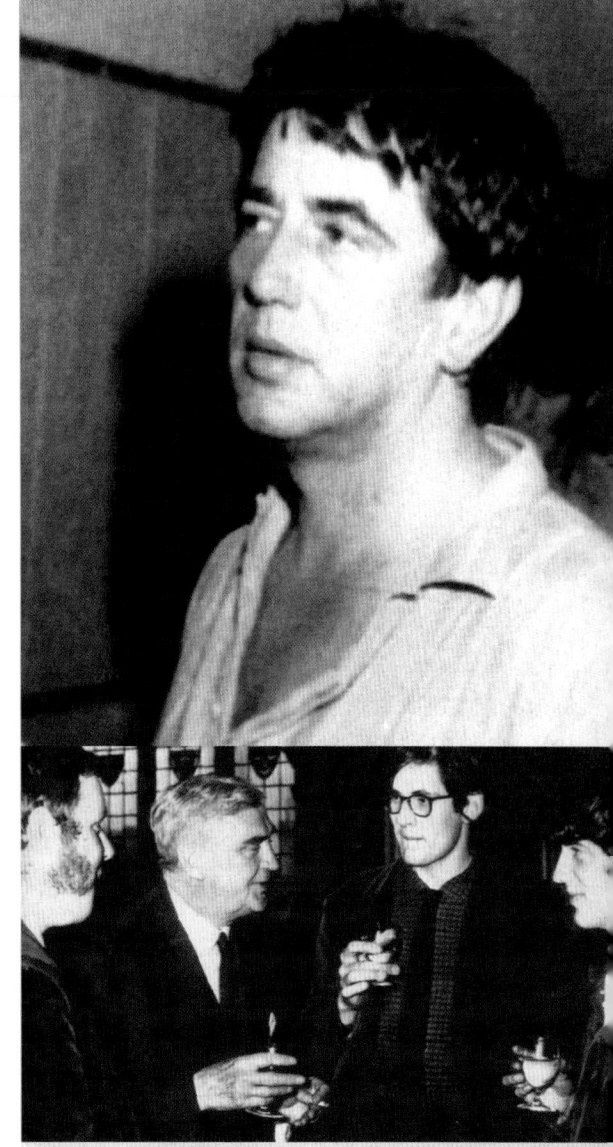

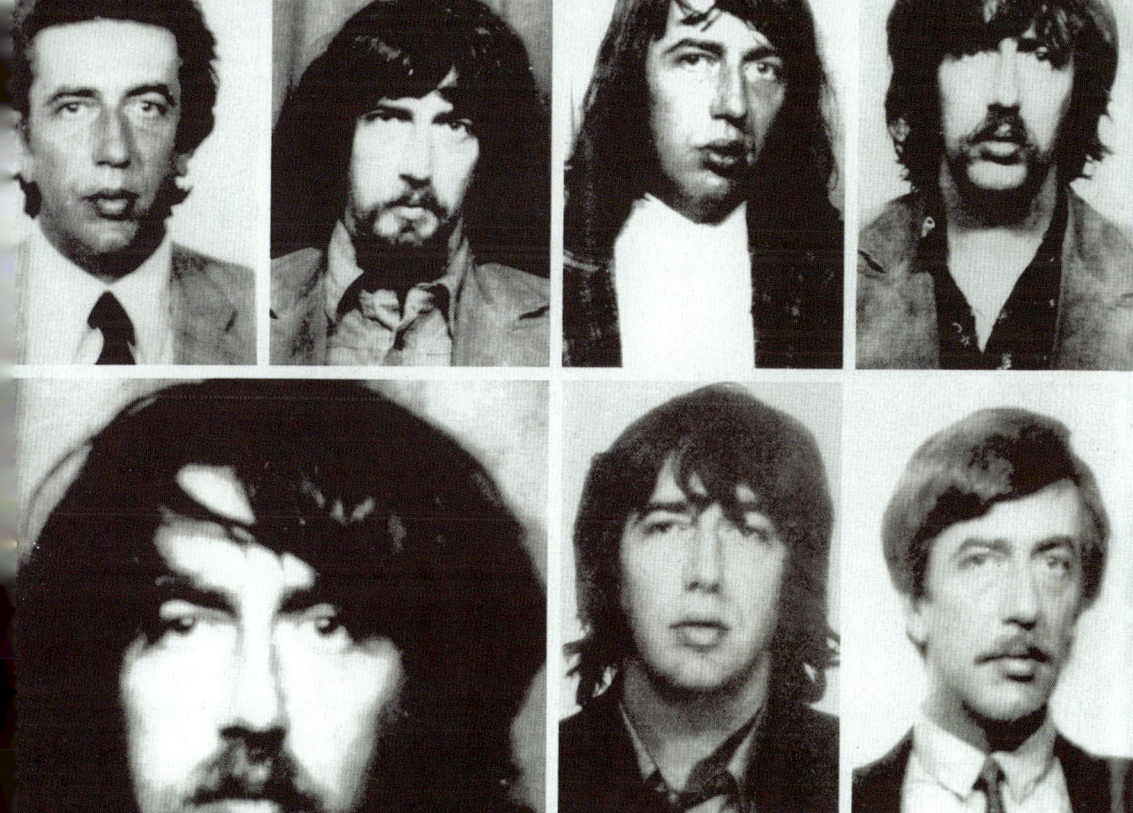

DR IN CHAINS
Worldwide net traps evil gang

THE man thought to head the world's biggest drugs ring was behind bars last night.

Earlier, 42-year-old Dennis Howard Marks had been led into court, in chains and under armed guard.

With him were his wife, Judith, and his henchman, fellow Briton Geoffrey Hugh Kenion, 46.

The three, arrested on Monday, were quizzed by an examining magistrate before being sent back to their cells on the Mediterranean holiday isle of Majorca.

By RAB ANDERSON and ED OWEN

officers from Scotland Yard, the United States Drug Enforcement Agency and a special team of Spanish anti-drug officers teamed up for the early morning raid on the Marks home.

There was no resistance. Marks and his 30-year-old wife were taken completely by surprise.

Surprise

In the sleepy police HQ at Palma, police were...

Tense: Kenion arrives to face an examining magistrate

Arrests

...marijuana plantations to the streets of Britain, the United States and anywhere else he could ply his sick trade.

...the world were holding 22 alleged members of the drugs ring.

They include 66-year-old American William Roger Reaves, arrested in Majorca three weeks ago.

Law officers in Miami, Florida have started extradition proceedings against him and the three others.

More arrests are expected in Britain by Scotland Yard detectives who helped to bust the...

PAGE 4 — DAILY MIRROR, Friday, April 18, 1975

WHERE IS MR MARKS?

vanished before an Old Bailey drug-smuggling trial has been interpreted as a link between an IRA drugs ring, the IRA Provisionals – the British Secret...

...old Howard Marks, days ago after claiming that landed him to become an...

...tectives to be a veritable member of the Secret Service that Marks sympathises with the IRA...

...of Balliol College, Oxford fear for his safety and close to his safety and was taken to an hotel in to keep his mouth...

...recalled in the drug world and...

...claimed to be with whom...

...'tives told: He was...with IRA

Mr Mystery slips back to Britain in secret

MARKS: Vanished before trial.

By TOM MERRIN and EDWARD LAXTON

STERY man oward Marks urned up in

9-year-old Oxford , who is alleged been the link een the British service, IRA gun and a Mafia ket, disappeared eve of an Old ial a year ago. oped bail of a multi- ound

Operation

aster £20m ' ring'

where he lived with year-old Mrs. A Man call

the mother of his year-old d Mifanwy H-

End of line for dr nlo

FORMER secret agent Howard Marks was jailed for three years yesterday for his part in a drug-smuggling operation.

A gang smuggled six loads of cannabis hidden in pop group loudspeakers into the United States. On the seventh run the drugs were detected by a "sniffer dog."

Marks, an Oxford graduate and former MI6 agent, said he got mixed up in the drugs plot while trying to infiltrate an IRA gun-running racket.

Racket

Passing sentence Old Bailey Judge Jame... to Marks's...

JAIL ROOF DEMO
1am news

RAMPAGING prisoners...

Daily

MONDAY, MAY...

SAS SECURITY MEN QUIZ THE FUGI

By RAYMOND RODGERS

intelligence were last night man of...

Britons s swoop on cannabis

The Sun
Monday, May 14, 1990 22p

Queen's cousin is a broke charlady

EXCLUSIVE

From GRAHAM DUDMAN in Tel Aviv

A COUSIN of the Queen is living in poverty in Israel... as a CHARLADY, The Sun can re...

EXPOSED
YARD CHIEF'S LINKS WITH DRUGS Mr BIG

WESTERN MAIL, FRIDAY, OCTOBER 9

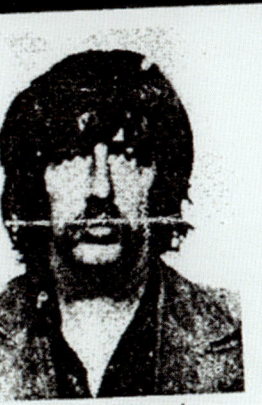

AND THE LINK IS…
Not a lot of people know this, but Howard Marks is responsible for the fact that I tour the world doing Audiences With Dave Courtney – so now you know who to blame!

Ronnie Biggs
The One That Got Away

FACTS

RONNIE BIGGS THE ONE THAT GOT AWAY

DAVE'S DODGY DOSSIER

Ronnie Biggs was an 'honest' low-level crook when he was asked by Bruce Reynolds to be in the gang to rob the Glasgow to London mail train. He was not involved in planning the robbery and his sole responsibility was to supply someone capable of driving a diesel train. Following his escape from Wandsworth Prison, he underwent painful plastic surgery to alter his appearance and fled to Australia. Tipped off about a possible arrest there, he travelled to Rio where his cover was eventually blown when an interview was hijacked by the police. Because he was about to father a Brazilian child, he was allowed residency. He returned to England in 2001 seriously ill.

HIS DODGIEST DAY

The old rope ladder over the wall trick never failed in the films and it never failed in real life for Ronnie Biggs. In fact it was so successful that a load of other cons managed to get up it and over the wall before the screws twigged. Let's just say that getaway car was a bit crowded that day.

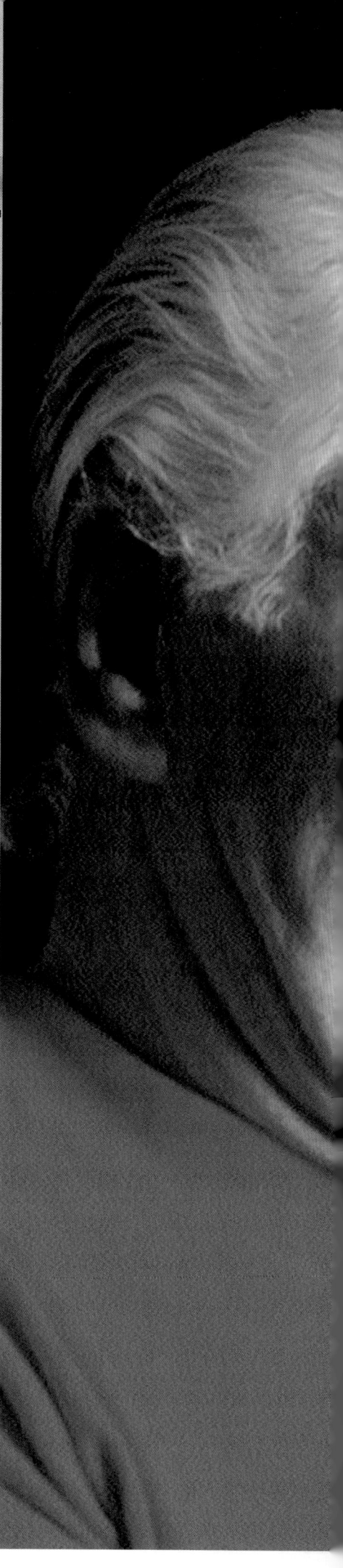

It's an era when if a bank job went wrong, the worst that would happen is a copper would chase you with a whistle.

> *If there's anything the police hate more than a criminal, it's a criminal hero. Look at me.* **DAVE**

Ronnie Biggs was never the brains of the Great Train Robbery – he weren't even the brawn – but he's the one we all remember, cos he's The One That Got Away.

I've seen a lot of Hollywood films that are more realistic than Ronnie's life – the things that happened to him just don't happen to normal people, do they? It's a proper dreamy story for anyone who's a bit naughty or anyone who's got someone inside. There's a real light at the end of the tunnel feeling when you look at Ron. When Bruce Reynolds was putting together his gang to hijack the Glasgow to London mail train and nick two and a half mill, he pulled in specialist chaps from all areas of crime. Everything was planned to the smallest detail like a proper military operation and worked out well in advance. He even went to the fucking trouble of buying a farmhouse near the crime scene so they could have a local base – which anyone who's ever bought a house will know ain't that much easier than knocking off a train-load of currency. The only thing left on Reynolds' shopping list was a bloke who could drive a diesel train – and he knew a man who knew a man.

So it were Ronnie who came up with a driver, and what a blinding success that turned out to be. Not. The whole heist went like clockwork and all Ronnie had to do was get his man into the driver's cab to replace the original driver who was nursing a sore head. But Ronnie's bloke couldn't do it (he couldn't find the funny handbrake they have on these trains) so he and Ronnie were told to fuck off back to the Land Rover to wait.

So Ronnie never actually hit anyone over the head, he never lifted a single bag from the train into the lorry, he never did fuck all, really. But he was still arrested as part of the gang and sent down to Wandsworth, via Leicester, which is the English equivalent of Alcatraz – but without the sea view.

Ron's only been in there ten minutes when he's decided to try to get out. No offence to the geezer, cos he's a lovely bloke an' that, but if Ronnie Biggs can escape from your prison, maybe it ain't as water-tight as it could be? You've got to remember this was an era where one Kray could visit his brother in prison and pretend to be him, so the other one could escape. It's an era when if a bank job went wrong, the worst that would happen is a copper would chase you with a whistle – and if he could find a police box on the corner, he might call some backup and so you might get tailed by a Wolsey.

So Ronnie's great plan was for this geezer to pull up in a van outside Wandsworth during an exercise bit, chuck a rope ladder over the wall while some chaps distracted the screws, and Ronnie'd hop over and in through the sunroof. As escape plans go, it's up there with tunnelling out of Germany with teaspoons, ain't it? You expect to see the old vaulting horse from the war films, it's that corny. It was never gonna work, was it? But it fucking did. It worked so well that not only did Ronnie and his mate get over the wall, but half a dozen other lags saw the opportunity and shinned up the ladder as well.

Apart from exposing the fact that Group Four couldn't have made a bigger cock-up of security, Ronnie escaping has actually stuck two fingers up at the authorities, ain't it? If there's anything the police hate more than a criminal, it's a criminal hero. Look at me: they couldn't give a toss about Dave Courtney while he was waving shooters at bank clerks, but as soon as I got a bit flash at Ronnie Kray's funeral and people started being interested in me, the authorities went, 'Shut that cunt down.' So even though Ronnie Biggs didn't really do that much in the actual crime, he was just one of the geezers who played Monopoly in the farm house while everyone got ready, the police leaked all these stories to the press about what a bad man he was so people would grass him up.

If someone's got popularity on their side then the chances of the police finding him are slim. It's the Robin Hood friend-of-the-masses thing. **DAVE**

That's actually an old police trick, if you're interested. If someone's got popularity on their side then the chances of the police finding him are slim. It's the Robin Hood friend-of-the-masses thing. So the police try to use the media to make people out to be worse than they are. When the IRA is doing well, for example, the whole country hides them. If the police come round, no Paddy will grass them up. So what the police do sometimes is let the call come in that tips them off that there's a bomb in Tesco's – and then do fuck all about it. Seriously, they are that calculating. The bomb goes off, kills a load of kids and now everyone hates the IRA and grasses them up.

With Ronnie it didn't really work, though. He's got more coverage than anyone I know, it was massive, blanket exposure for weeks, but it achieved bugger all. He got his face all surgery'd up so no one would recognize him, then sodded off to Australia with his family for a few years. Then when the heat got a bit strong there – and I'm not talking about the sunshine – he nipped over to Rio.

Ronnie's life over there was out of this world. He had his own private swimming pool, two rottweilers looking after his house. There was a constant stream of people all around the world who were well-wishers. Anyone with half a bollock would love him and help him and give him money or cover for him. He's just a fucking hero. So it was a great honour for me to be invited over to celebrate his 70th birthday a few years back, and I got to know him very well. It was the fucking horniest thing in the world, just being in a room with my mates Roy Shaw, Bruce Reynolds and all the remaining Great Train Robbers – including Ronnie Biggs! I was just sitting there going, 'Wow!' I didn't know Ronnie at the time, but I'd written and corresponded with him and a lot of my friends had gone over there and visited him. We're the same circle of people, if you know what I mean. If Stanley Matthews was alive, David Beckham would know him.

Anyway, cos I was friends with Roy Shaw and Bruce Reynolds and Mickey Biggs, they thought I'd add a bit of colour to the party, and they was fucking spot on. I went over there with a load of plastic police helmets, we did a bit of karaoke (and what a fucking surprise package Roy Shaw turned out to be with a mike in his hands) and I brought a letter from my old mate Charlie Bronson. I won't reveal exactly what it said, but it contained the advice 'never back into a Scotsman wearing a kilt' and a few of Charlie's unique pictures. You won't find it in Clinton Cards, mate, put it that way.

Cos Ronnie had no income when he first got there, the authorities smoked him out with a bit of money. He said he'd sell his story to the Daily Express for 50 grand, but, halfway through the interviews, in walks Slipper of the Yard and he's carted off for extradition. Luckily for Ron, the Brazilian courts have gone, 'He's got a boy with a Brazilian woman so he can legally live here.' What a fucking touch that was.

But once it became common knowledge that Ronnie was living like a king in Rio even though he didn't have two bob to rub together, and he couldn't be deported, certain people tried a few naughty little tricks to get him back. There's a really beautiful story that mercenaries went over there and kidnapped him. At the time, kidnapping in Brazil was everywhere. They were kidnapping children and only asking for 500 quid or they'd kill the kid. It don't sound much, but everyone can raise 500 quid so they all paid up. They killed a few kids to start with, which made sure every mum found 500 quid within half an hour. Tramps would get a bus 80 miles, nick a kid and then call up the parents and go, 'Oi.'

Anyone with half a bollock would love him and help him and give him money or cover for him.

THE WORLD CHRONICLE
BIGGS ELUDES YARD AGAIN!
olice to
all for
andom
ests
Petrol price rise turns away many motorists
Govt hopes to cut jail wage bill by

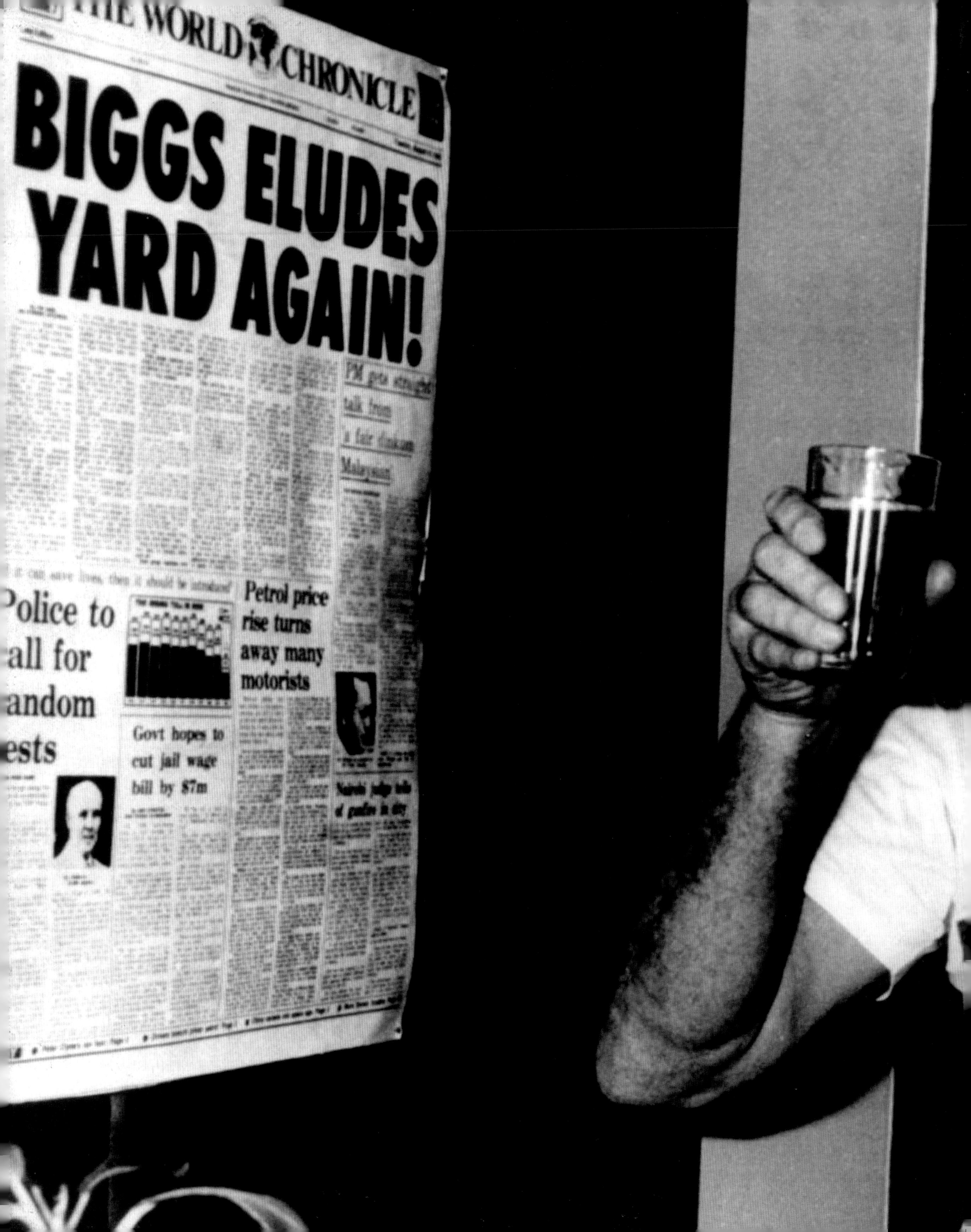

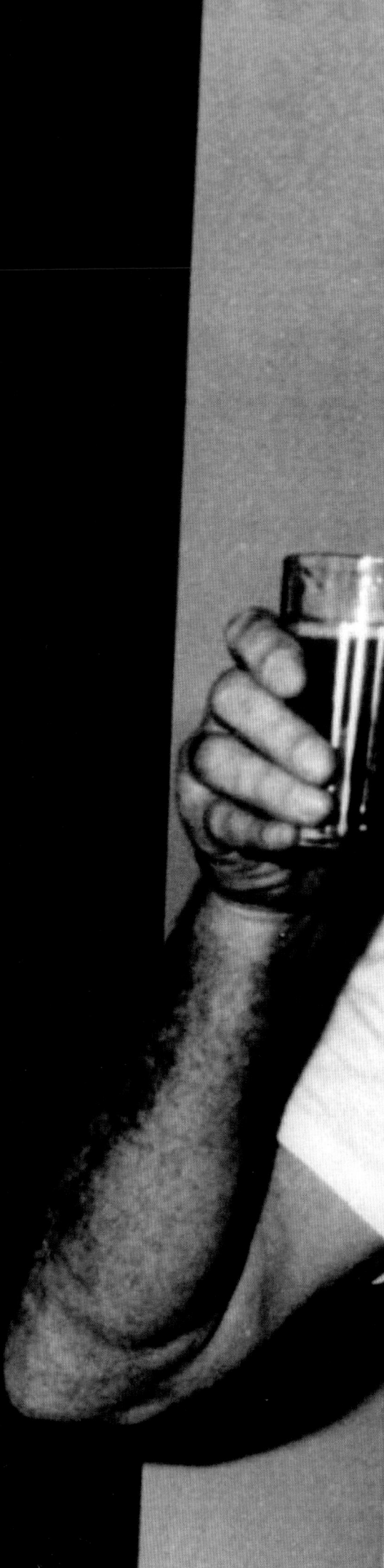

Mickey Biggs was a famous pop star in Brazil at the time. He was the Robbie Williams of Rio. So when his dad went missing, he went on TV and made such a heart-wrenching plea that there was action. He went, 'You've allowed some other country to come into Brazil and kidnap my dad, put him on a boat to a British frigate and show off about it in the papers…' It was like Robbie Williams saying it now. The whole country went into uproar and the Brazilian navy was sent out to intercept this boat and bring Ronnie back. That's sexy, ain't it?

Mickey's a great kid. Him and his dad are like royalty in Brazil so it was an honour to have him in my film Hell to Pay. He plays a screw at Wandsworth prison – can you see where I'm going with this? – and he says to two lags, 'Sorry, boys, got to run – I've got a train to catch.' Up yours, Old Bill.

AND THE LINK IS…
It was a great honour for me to be invited over to celebrate Ronnie's 70th birthday a few years back, and I got to know him very well. We're the same circle of people, if you know what I mean. If Stanley Matthews was alive, David Beckham would know him.

Well, there you have it.

Ten blokes to look up to and ten right shady geezers to give your kids nightmares. But like I said at the start, as far as I'm concerned most of the chaps mentioned in the book are heroes to me, it's just that some are real and some are made-up. Apart from one or two, they all either fall into the 'good baddy' or 'bad goody' category, which in my book makes them all right – and considering this is my book, what I say goes. But I'd say they're all blokes you could learn something from – even if it's just 'don't get fucking caught!'

But as heroes go, there are plenty of others in my life (and yes, some of these could technically be described as villains too), so here are a few names. They might mean fuck all to you, but they mean everything to me so they're getting a shout:

My Mum, Teresa Courtney; My Stormylicious; George at the Tardis, Clerkenwell, London; Nick Reynolds and the Cons to Icons Exhibition; Sunny Side Up, Charlton; Karisma; Skin Two; Pure; Rob's Barbers, Forest Hill; Leraze Hair Salon, Portsmouth; Piers Hernu and Front; Capital FM; 1 FM; Millennium FM; News of the World; Sunday Sport; The Voice; Andy Harrison and Delilah Amis; South London Press; Pete Conway and Robbie Williams; Darren Gough; Tony Thompson – Gangland Britain; Jocelyn Bain Hogg; Combat; Nodd, Hector, James and Cyrus @ Ministry Magazine; Chris @ Skinhead and Scooter Magazine; Marcus Georgio and Marc One Security; Titan Security; Brian Adams and Hatch Farm Studios; Mojo; Caesar the Geezer; Mike Osmond and the Naughty Boys; Karaoke Chas; Huey; Aphrodite; Carl 'Tuff Enuff' Brown; DJ Beau Courtney and Blood; Mr Normski; Danielle Montana; MC Cream and Dominic Spreadlove; Mickey Finn; DJ Hurley; DJ Nathan Healey; Huey and the Fun Lovin' Criminals; Stereophonics; Gary G; One Nation and Garage Nation; Clive Button and Lee Patrick; Dave Courtney's Web Designers: Mal Vango, Lion Design, Steve and Paul; Victoria and Rich; Vanessa Feltz; Zo and Zane; MCPSG; Mark and Jude Coventry; Pasquelle; Maria from Cassidy's; my Ria; Gordon and Juliette; Gerry and Kate; Linda and Frank; Pierre and Helen; John Gillingham; Geraldine and Gail; Liam and Yvette; Francis Bacon RIP; Simon Weston; Les Ferdinand; Neil Hamilton; Max Beasley; Lyndsey Marsh; Dianne and Chris Hackett; John and Kay; John Disley; Diane and Jim, Hayling Island; Diane, Reece and Lulu; Snoop Dogg; HRH Jodie Marsh; Melinda Messenger; Jamie Oliver; James Whale; Welsh Bernie; Adrian Sington and Eleanor Maxfield at Virgin; Jeff Hudson; all the Scousers, the Geordies, the Paddies, the Jocks and the Taffs and all Bike Presidents everywhere; Sir Paul Condon; HRH the Prince of Wales and Harry and Wills; Dick Emery – ooh, you are awful but I like you; Malcolm McLaren; and all at Her Majesty's pleasure.

THE KIDS

Lots of love from Dave: Genson; Drew; Levi; Chelsea; Courtney 'My Lully Girl' and Beau. Joel; Noel; Brogan; Delaney; Bianca; Aspen; John; Brook; Big Jordan; Little Jordan; Brinie; Connor; Tiona; Kayleigh and Ben; Rachel, Zoe; Tommy; Nyasha; Maria and Pedzi.

MEN OF INSPIRATION

So good they're in here twice: Joey Pyle; Roy 'Pretty Boy' Shaw; Freddie Foreman; Tony Lambrianou RIP; Chris Lambrianou; Ronnie Biggs; Bruce Reynolds; Howard Marks; Charlie Bronson; Charlie Richardson; Johnny Nash; Muhammad Ali; Sir Winston Churchill; Ho Chi Minh; Ernesto 'Che' Guevara; Niccolo Machievelli; King Arthur and the Knights of the Round Table.

THE HELL TO PAY CAST & CREW

Eamonn O'Keefe; Roberto Gomez; Austin Vernon; Malcolm Martin; Brian Hovmand; Nicola Fletcher; Kevin Crace; Austin Vernon; Will Chown, Oliver Manzi, 'Andreas'; Shoot–for–the–Stars Ltd; Alistair Macfarlane, Ross Perkin RM (Ret'd); Phil Anderson, Ross Anderson; Micky Goldtooth, Robbie Drake; Julian MacDonald; Sam Matthews; Kerrie MacDonald; Ben Beaumont; Anne Foged; Roberto Gomez; Conan McStay; Dominic Selby; Drew Hosie; Rhiann McAllister; Barnaby Kirk, Babs Gadenne, Andy Biggs; Rami Bartholdy; Satu Ellard; Steve Bosnich, David Brady; Dave Smithers, Darko Mocilnikar; John Santa Cruz; Kevin Courtney; Andy Bedford; Frances Williams; Constantine Georgiou; Darren Knight; Danilo Gomez–Cravitz; Anthony Brown, Jeremy Bailey; Malcolm Martin, Brendan Carr. Lars, Tim, Matt and Brett – the Rancid boys. Norris Da Boss Windross, J Offenbach, The Business and Steve Whale, Elliott Sagor and Laurence Adeokun, Tricky, Rancid and Lars Fredericksen, Izzy Asco'ta, Joski, Celloman, Sean Flowers, Extreme Music; Lounge Audio Post; Metro Broadcast VMI and Video Europe, London; Satisfaction, London; Peach Ideas, London; NTL and Video Europe, London; NTL – Barnaby and Babs; The Crucifixion by Ronnie Kray courtesy of Phil Mordew and 'John'; Short Stories, Commercial Road, London; Dock Gate 20, Southampton; Cohibas, Monte Cristo and Romeo y Julieta; Andy Gardner, Jim's Garage, Teddy and Lenny Webb and Colin Gray; TC; Richard at M1 Print.

John Altman; Angela Bassett; 'Nasty' Nick Bateman; Matt Bearman, Andy Beckwith; Leah Bedford; Jim Benson; Michael Biggs; Sir Charlie Breaker; 'Cowboy' Brian; Gillian Brewer; Kelly Burgess; Garry Bushell; Sue Carpenter; Albert Chapman; Choo & JC Mac; 'Kelly'; Peter Conway; Chantel Cummins; Julius Francis; Ian 'The Machine' Freeman; Peter Friel; Owen Gardener; Ian Golding; Jo Guest; Jez; Gary Hailes; Martin Hancock; Paul Haines; Steve Holdsworth; Helen Keating; Jamie Kent; Jimmy 'The Gent' Kent; Dave Laine; Tony Lambrianou; Dave Legeno; Francine Lewis; Steve Lowe; Tony Maile; Mark and Kevin; Malcolm Martin; Roxanne Martin; Johnny McGee; Brendan McGirr; Mark Morrison; Billy Murray; Kelly Noyes; Tony Oakey; Eamonn O'Keefe; Jamie O'Keefe; Lucy O'Keefe; Cass Pennant; Mickey Pugh; Joey Pyle; Joey Pyle Jr; John Pyle; 'Bald' Rob; Marcus Redwood; Nick Reynolds; Adam Saint; Steve Sadler; Scorpion; 'Scouse'; Roy 'Pretty Boy' Shaw; Lou Szulc; Tarkan; Terry Turbo; Scott Welch; Steve Whale; Wolfie; Seymour Young.

THE HOODS

Wish; Gary Love; Rickie O'Keefe; Mark Ives; Trevor Mailey; Warren Attitude; Panay Ioutou; Keith Winn; Alex Reed; Bez; Panos Sotirou; Boxer Lester; Adrian 1 and 2; Big Lloyd; Gary Collins; Micky Roth; Colin; Syringes Tony; Rob Sylvester; Mark Hall; Adrian Doughty; Jamie MacDonald; Vic Bishop; Big John x 5; Big Frank x 5; Ken Alexanders; Rich Luff; John Corbet; Andy Gardner; Rob Scott; Adi Woods; Matt Tobin; Le Grande Danoir; Nice Guy Eddie; Alfie Fitness; Mark Lodge; Andre the Wrestler; Dean Coldwell; Tony Maloney; Jack Holman; Martin Lovelock; Andy The Mill; Rob Oakes; Simon Oakes; Jaz; Ricky English; The Six Bend Trap Crew; Jackson Kennedy; Peter Watson; Faz; Frankie Baby; Bernie Davies; Chops; Patrick Courtney; Folkestone Matt; Joey Moore; Big Barry x 3; Pete Henshaw; Andrew Brown; Paul Hughes; Zombie; Christian Kiwi; Big Geoff; Andy Kiwi; Wayne Pursell; Dave Drum; Steve Raith; Damian 1 and 2; Sheffield Ben; Boo; Reece Huxford; Antoni O'Shea; Tank; Danny; Dave Thurston; Musher; Baz; Dukie; Danny Dolittle; Mark Peters; Rubber Ron; Stormin' Norman; Suda; Bob Tanner; Big Ern, Danny Cheltenham; Tim Tivey; Jullian White; Paddy; Sheffield Daz; Nick Moorcroft; The RSM; Big Lee; Fat Lawrence; Manny Clark; Neil Wolf and the Tally Ho Crew; Ebo; Bexley Don; Bexley Al, Jay; Costas; Handsome John; Mark Piano; Colin Dunne; Lance Clark; Jaws; The Old Twins; Bismarck; Winkle; Pard; Dave Hurst; Big Dave x 3; Posh John; Chino; Del; Paul and Aaron Stone; Elliot Clark; Neil O'Brien; Fred Batt; Clive McGee; Stretch; Tonbridge Richard; Jamie Taylor; John Farnell; John Boy; Scotty; Geoff Vines; Gary Vines; Paul Haynes; Rico; Lennie Lucas; Fetish Alan; Sam Sharma; Big Mark x 5; Jamie Taylor; Dallas; Ray Steele; Mark Ives; Elpae Georgiou; Brooklyn John; Junior; Handsome Rod; Colin x 4; Kenny Panda; Roy Schnell; Lox; Micky Goldsmith; Juror; Steve; Ken Alexanders; H; Simon Rayner; John Corbett; Chris Hammer; Boogie; Rick Hards; Bruzzie; Shovels; Mad Brian Dival; Dingus McGee; Scully; Fat Lawrence; Woody; Jason Willis; Birmingham John; Big Wayne; Francisco; Fly; Boris; John Tom; Kevin O'Dowd; Rob Andrews; USA Johnny; Louie; Jimmy Cook; Mark McCarthy (Six Bend Trap); John Armour; Jamie Scunthorpe; Mark Fish – Mr Scunthorpe; Sooty and Weep; Big Pete from Pasha; The Animal; Joey Stretch; Pilchard; Linford; James Cohen; Leo; Lee Cross; Perry Benson; Reading Les; Grub Smith; Craig; Birmingham Keith; Lambross; Darren Hearn; Mr T; Mickey Jackson; Steve Foster; Rob from Milton Keynes; Big Ron; Rooster Ian; Mohammed; Mario; Gary Baron; Timmy Abet; Bernie Lee; Paul Scarface; Mick Chapman; Tim Newton; Kiwi and Terry Mallett; Carl Beatty; Busbie; Noel Moyston; Outcast Phil; Rob Hanson; Warrior; Colin Robertson; Byrd Byron; Lee Philips; Bruno Draper; Bradley from the Studio; Boyzie @ Ministry; Black Dave; Dax; James Weatherer; Phil Organ; Terry Currie; Irish Dave McConnell; Tony Simpson; Trevor Tanner; Keith Walker; Lee Murray the Main Man; Roberto Lozano; Gavin the Gatemaker – my Randall to his Hopkirk; Matt Ridley; Peter Fen; Lawrence and the Redz; Ayatollah Massive; Scots Rory; Harry Marsden; Rino; Big Chewy; John Edwards; Cecil @ Chinawhite's; Stilks; Sting; Stuart from Fulham; Roy and the Dirt Track Boys; Tel Boy; Tally from Tenerife; Eddie from Fulham; Tim @ UB40; Wolves Paul; Fisher Boxing Club; Tony Macmahon; Steve Hooper; Vince from Birmingham; Jay; Big Keg; Big Dennis; Big Don; No Neck Nick; Zac; Zeus; Zig; Chey; Big Ray; Chris Collins; Mark Epstein; Gart Abnet.

THE HOODETTES

Sabrina Libertucci; Holly Thomas; Clare Redman; Annie Deacin Foster; Bella Thekla Roth; Clarellen James; Lisa Henfrey; Ria Jaggard; Sue Moore; Tracy Fenada; Victoria Kay; Daisy Kay; Courtney de Courtney; Bonnie, Marsha; Welsh Helen; Little Tasha; Di; Dionne; Drew; Nadia; Lady Carol; Terri Currie; Leah; Bev 1, 2 and 3; Autumn and EJ; Loretta; Lex; Ruth Lawrence; Bev and Gemma; Welsh Paula; Natasha Taylor; Staffy; Safi; Sad Happy; Ellie; Yasmin; Sugar; Lartey; Tess Courtney; Susan Courtney; Tania Bushell; Denice; Jacky Carr; Claire McNamara; Kate McNamara; Isabella O'Shea; Terri Georgiou; Neke Georgiou; Jessica Georgiou-Cross; Sister Beckford; Summer; Katie Campbell; Kat; Lorna Elliott; Ministry Pam; Fru Jaggard; Auntie Myrtle; Caroline Benn; Kaz; Lyndsey Joins; Jane Courtney; Lynn Cooley; Carol Jenkins; Alisha Kusabi; Sue Pyle; Angela Archeleta; Debbie Tucker; Tara Tucker; Baby Angel Pyle; Little Jenny; Candy Floss; Karen Giorgio; Ann Johnstone; Sally Farmer; Caleb Giorgio; Ita; Barbie; Jean; Charlotte Ratcliffe; Blossom; Sandy Farnell; Danielle Elliott; Bev; Mo; Chantelle; Kerry; Connie; Lulu; Elsie Davie RIP.

AND THE REST

John Pound's Scrapyard; Portsmouth; Jam @ Manhattan's, Woolwich; Gilly @ Gambinos, Gravesend; Lou and Tony Aquarium, Old Street, London; The Dusterman; 'Cowboy' Brian; Beiderbeck's, Portsmouth; Park Tavern Boxing Club, Tooting; Sir Micky Colby; Chris and Sue Vernon; Pierce and Michelle Vernon; Elsie and Jack Vernon; Oliver Vernon RIP; Mirza Fur; Armando and Jayne Gomez-Martin; Catrina Gomez-Martin; Joan Dybowski; Lis and Helmuth Hovmand; Peter Hamden @ LipSyncPost, London; Ian Diaz and Julian Boote @ 712 Collective; Ali Catterall; Barry Keefe; Phil Ballard; Steven Moxley; Matthew Owen; Adrian Gardiner; James Pearson; Mitch @ Laughing Buddha, London; Michael @ Jerry's Members Club, Soho, London; Simon Wells; Paul Kennedy @ Inside, London; Premier Despatch; Belle Stennett and the staff at the Dome Cinema, Worthing; John @ the Tower Club, Littlehampton; Eze and Seamus @ the Crown, Littlehampton; Ali Jacko; Maximillian; And to all the major players in Britain's underworld.

And a BIG shout to all the doormen and organisers at: Ministry of Sound; Hippodrome; Stringfellows; K-Bar, Chelsea; Chinawhite's; Isola, Knightsbridge; Buzz Bar; Ronnie Scott's; Bagley's; SE24; Caesars, Streatham; Time and Envy, Portsmouth; Submission; Atlantic Bar; the Ten Rooms; Titanic; Limelight; Propaganda; Stage 3; Sophisticats; the Champagne Bar, Twickenham; Elvis Chipshop; Torture Garden; Driscoll's; Gatecrashers; and all the table top dancers in the country.

DAVE COURTNEY OBE

Altman, John 87
Angels With Dirty Faces (1938) 20-27, 30
Anselmi, Albert 16

Bandello, Rico 28-35
Barrie, John 'Ian' 99
Beckham, David 64
Bender, Ronnie 99
Big Chris 76-83
Biggs, Mickey 87, 130, 170, 173
Biggs, Ronnie 114, 166-73
Blair, Tony 15
Bogart, Humphrey 20
Brando, Marlon 34-43
Bronson, Charles 150-7, 170
Bugner, Joe 86
Bushell, Gary 87

Caan, James 36
Cagney, James 20-7, 30
Capone, Al 8, 12-9, 23, 32, 46, 91
Cardinella, Salvatore 30
Clary, Julian 86
Connery, Sean 89
Conteh, John 87
Corleone, Don 36-43

De Niro, Robert 60-7
Dellacroce, Armond 122
Dennis, Teddy 145
Douglas, Kirk 25

Edwards, Buster 145
Escobar, Pablo 11

Faulkner, Lisa 86
Foreman, Freddie 101, 130, 142-9
Fraser, Frankie 16, 107, 114, 130, 146, 153

Gambino Family 118-25
Godfather, The (1972 & 1974) 36-45
Goodfellas (1990) 54-9
Gotti, John 118-25
Great Train Robbery 126-33, 166-73
Guest, Jo 87
Guevara, Che 11
Guinness Book of Records 15

Haeems, Ralph 43, 99
Hancock, Martin 87
Hays Production Code 31
Heat (1995) 60-7
Hell To Pay (2005) 84-91
Hill, Henry 52-9

Jackson, Samuel L. 68, 71
Janus, Samantha 86
Jones, Vinnie 76-83

Keitel, Harvey 73
Krays, the 15, 16, 32, 43, 57, 87, 94-101, 105, 107, 107, 113, 114, 145

Lambrianou, Chris 145
Lambrianou, Tony 99, 114, 145
Legano, Dave 87
Liotta, Ray 52-9
Little Caesar (1931) 25-35
Lock, Stock & Two Smoking Barrels (1998) 76-83
Longford, Lord 154

Malone, Dave 84-91
Marks, Howard 158-95
McCauley, Neil 60-7
McLean, Lenny 79, 114, 134-41
McVitie, Jack 'The Hat' 94, 145
Mitchell, Frank 142, 145-6
Montana, Tony 44-51
Moran, Bugsy 12
Moran, Nick 86
Murray, Billy 87, 89

Nash, Johnny 112, 113, 145
Noye, Kenny 112

Pacino, Al 30, 36, 38, 39, 44-51, 60, 63, 64, 65, 67
Pesci, Joe 56
Pfeiffer, Michelle 48-9
Pine, Wilf 123
Pulp Fiction (1995) 68–75
Pyle, Joey 89, 110–7, 137

Reynolds, Bruce 116, 126-32, 169, 170
Richardsons, the 102-9, 113
Ritchie, Guy 76, 78-9, 80
Robben, Arjen 64
Robinson, Edward G. 28-35
Rocos, Cleo 86

Scalise, John 16
Scarface (1983) 44-51
Seaman, David 86
Shaw, Roy 87, 114, 134-41, 170
St Valentine's Day Massacre (1929) 12, 23
Sullivan, Rocky 20-7

Tarantino, Quentin 71, 75
'Teflon Don, The' 118-25
'Ten Commandments, The' 23
Travolta, John 68-75

Vega, Vincent 68-75
Warnes, Austin 15
Whitehead, Cornelius 'Connie' 99
Willis, Bruce 73